PRAYER AS A PLACE
CHARLES BELLO SPIRITUALITY THAT TRANSFORMS

HGM Publishing
a division of Heart of God Ministries
3720 S. Hiwassee Rd., Choctaw, OK 73020

I

Printed in the United States of America
Published by HGM Publishing
3720 S. Hiwassee Rd.
Choctaw, OK 73020-6128

Layout and cover design: Justin Falk
Chapter title artwork & illustrations: Bjorn Bauer, www.bjornbauerart.com

FOR DIANNA

C O N T E N T S

SECTION 1 FOLLOWING CHRIST INWARD
01   AN INVITATION AND A WARNING
02   SPIRITUAL DISCIPLINES AS A PLACE TO ENCOUNTER JESUS
03   SPIRITUAL DISCIPLINES AS A PLACE TO ENCOUNTER OURSELVES
04   OUR SPIRITUAL JOURNEY: CULTIVATING AN INNER LIFE THAT
      SUSTAINS OUTWARDLY-FOCUSED LIVING

SECTION 2 ANCIENT PATHS TO CHRISTIAN SPIRITUALITY
05   CONTEMPLATIVE PRAYER AS A PLACE
06   DEVELOPING A SABBATICAL RHYTHM
07   CENTERING PRAYER: RESTING IN GOD
08   THE EXAMEN: PAYING ATTENTION TO GOD
09   JOURNALING AS A PLACE OF PRAYER AND TRANSFORMATION
10   WALKING WITH GOD
11   LECTIO DIVINA: ENCOUNTERING GOD IN THE BIBLE

SECTION 3 MAKING A LASTING CHANGE
12   A TRACK TO RUN ON
13   ENCOUNTERING GOD TOGETHER: PROCESSING YOUR INNER
      LIFE WITH OTHERS

01   LECTIO DIVINA: THEMES
02   LECTIO DIVINA: OUTLINE
03   RECOMMENDED RESOURCES FOR THE INNER LIFE

ACKNOWLEDGMENTS

When I was in my early thirties, I had been pastoring for only a few years. I had made many of the mistakes that young, inexperienced pastors make – I preached too long, thought all my ideas were inspired by God, had boundless energy and enthusiasm that I mistook for the anointing of the Holy Spirit, had little patience for those who were not one hundred percent behind me, and believed that I would not make the same mistakes as other leaders. (I not only repeated many of their mistakes, I even made some new ones on my own.)

I had been a pastor for about five years when I was invited to lunch by a couple a little older than me. I had a tremendous love and respect for them both. They were very dedicated parents, loyal members of the church, and very supportive of me and my wife. But I had noticed for months that they seemed to be drifting from the church, so I wasn't surprised when, after some small talk, they shared that they believed that God was "moving them on." I told them how much I appreciated their love and support over the years, and I asked if they were thinking about being a part of another new church plant.

The man responded before he had a chance to edit his words. "I don't think we have the energy to raise another pastor," he said. Immediately, both he and his wife were embarrassed, but I laughed and genuinely thanked them for raising me. They continue to be friends.

In my early years of parenting, I heard that, "Parents don't raise children, children raise parents." I think that the same can be said of churches. Pastors don't grow churches, churches grow pastors. I will be forever grateful for those men and women who believed in us and joined with my wife and me as we sought to partner with Christ and his mission in the world. Oklahoma City Vineyard, thank you for helping to grow us up.

Special thanks to my family. Being a pastor is hard; being a pastor's kid is harder still. Nathan, Laura, Emily, Joseph, Levi and Jean-Luc, I love you all. You have done a great job of raising parents.

Special thanks to my daughter Laura Bauer and good friend Jeanie Gillham for reading over my early drafts and giving me much needed input, and to Audrey Colwell for serving me as an editor. Her editing skills and patience have made this book much more accessible.

But most of all, I want to thank my wife. Dianna has been my greatest fan and strongest critic. Her probing questions, listening ear and insightful comments keep me honest. We married young and shared the joys and trials of maturing together. I will always be grateful to you for your love and companionship.

SECTION 1
FOLLOWING CHRIST INWARD

C H A P T E R 1

AN INVITATION AND A WARNING

Those whom I love I rebuke and discipline. So be earnest, and repent. Here I am! I stand at the door and knock. If anyone hears my voice and opens the door, I will come in and eat with him, and he with me. To him who overcomes, I will give the right to sit with me on my throne, just as I overcame and sat down with my Father on his throne.
Revelations 3:19 – 21

In 1994, I was in prayer, asking God to empower me for ministry, when I heard him whisper in my heart, *If you don't let me love you, you won't finish the race.* I pondered this statement for a while. It sounded like both an invitation and a warning. I had been pastoring for more than 10 years. I had preached on the love of God many times. In fact, I had a reputation for being a very loving and kind person.

I asked God, *How do I let you love me?* He responded with a memory of me holding one of my children in my arms. My child was not doing anything but resting in my arms, letting me love him. God seemed to be saying that he wanted me to do the same with him – simply rest in him, do nothing but let him love me. So I began to set aside time every day to simply lie on the floor or make myself comfortable in an overstuffed easy-chair and invite God to come and love me.

After a few months of this practice, I was asking God the Father for more passion for his Son, when I heard him whisper in my heart, *You don't need more passion for Jesus. You need to know his passion for you.* This revolutionized my understanding of Christianity. This seemed to echo the words of the apostle John, "This is love: not that we loved God, but that he loved us" (1 John 4:10). I began to devote an hour or so a day to being with God and letting him love me. In the process, I found myself refreshed and recharged.

In the months that followed, I found myself reading Dallas Willard's *The Spirit of the Disciplines.* His assertion was that in order to be an authentic follower of Jesus, one needs to practice the disciplines that Jesus practiced. His premise resonated deep within me.

> We can become like Christ by doing one thing – by following him in the overall style of life he chose for himself. If we have faith in Christ, we must believe that he knew how to live. We can, through faith and grace, become like Christ by practicing the types of activities he engaged in, by arranging our whole lives around the activities he himself practiced in order to remain constantly at home in fellowship of his Father.
>
> What activities did Jesus practice? Such things as solitude and silence, prayer, simple and sacrificial living, intense study and meditation upon God's Word and God's ways, and service to others.[1]

As I began practicing the disciplines myself, I began teaching them as well. I made the classic mistake of simply seeing spiritual disciplines as activities rather than the means for creating a space to be encountered by God. I soon found out that adding more activities to an already busy schedule is a recipe for failure.

I shared my practice of letting God love me with an older pastor that I respected, and he seemed to roll his eyes. Something inside of me felt a little embarrassed. Soon the busyness and responsibility of ministry began to take up my time again. My practice of simply resting in God's love began to be pushed aside for more immediate things. It didn't take long for the practice of resting to disappear, and the other spiritual disciplines also fell away.

The decade that followed was filled with ministry and service. Our church was part of a larger movement that was experiencing an outpouring of the Holy Spirit that was bringing renewal and salvation to tens of thousands around the world.

Along with the renewal came controversy and criticism. We also saw thousands of young people reached in our community through a coffee house ministry we started called The Outer Café. We were on the local news. Other churches from around the country began contacting us about how to run outwardly-focused coffee houses. In the process I wore out my family and church. We saw many people saved, healed and delivered of demonic oppression, and equipped for ministry through short-term ministry trips to Cambodia, Malaysia, Germany, Switzerland, Austria, Holland, Romania, Slovakia and Mexico.

During the next 10 years we purchased a church building, experimented with a number of different congregational systems, took the church through a couple of major renovation projects, I finished graduate school, had a number of close relationships break down, had my church leadership team quit on me and leave the church, and raised up a new leadership team. My wife retired from her midwifery career to give more of her time to working alongside me in leading the church. And did I mention that we were raising our six children and that their teenage years were proving to be a challenge? For me, this decade is a blur.

In 2004, at 50 years old, I found myself at a retreat for burned-out pastors and their wives. I was there, not because I thought I was burned out, but because I knew my wife was not doing very well. She had been on antidepressant medication for almost a year, and I knew that I had to do something to get her back on her feet.

But at the retreat I began to acknowledge the fact that I was struggling, too. My energy level was at an all-time low. There was a deep pool of sadness within me that I was afraid to look at. As I looked around my community, I could see young pastors growing their churches while I was struggling just to keep the people I had. I found myself facing old sins I had long since thought I had overcome. And to be honest, I had thought I would be more successful at this point in my life. But I felt it was too late for a career change. If you had asked me how I was doing, I would have responded with, "Great! But things could always be better," and then run through a list of wonderful things I saw God doing.

I hated the idea of attending a retreat, but we'd been invited by our good friend, Judy Davids. Judy is a missionary, counselor and educator. She'd been commissioned by our denomination to develop retreats for burned-out pastors and their spouses. Sitting around and navel-gazing was not attractive to me; it seemed like an extreme waste of time. To make matters worse, this was a ten-day retreat. Ten days without a computer, ten days of no cell phone, ten days with no outside contact, and ten days with no ministry. Looking around at the other couples present, I wondered how many of the pastors were there for their depressed wives as well.

A couple of days into the retreat, as I started to slow down, I began to suspect that I might be in trouble. There was an assignment to go off by ourselves and invite Jesus into the deepest parts of ourselves. We were to journal our conversation. I hated journaling; I had dozens of journals under my bed, all beginning and ending within the first weeks of January. I was a total failure at keeping journals.

As I pondered my assignment to invite Jesus into the deepest parts of my life, I was startled to discover that I did not want Jesus in the deepest parts of my life. He was knocking at the door, and I did not want to let him in. I found myself bargaining with him. I told him that I wanted to remain a Christian, I would continue to be a faithful husband and loyal pastor, but, in my heart of hearts, I no longer wanted him that close. I no longer trusted him. This revelation shocked me. I sat there thinking, *I am a pagan! I am a pastor with the heart of a pagan!* I knew that this had not always been the case, but there I was, with more than 20 years of ministry behind me, working as hard as I knew how, doing it on my own, and no longer trusting God. I had seen the power of God touch others, but where was the power of God to save me? Christianity had become a heavy yoke.

My façade began to crumble. My wife was burned out, and I was in denial. In fact, I discovered that I was not only in burn-out mode myself, but I had emotionally shut down. I had lost my ability to be happy, sad or angry. In order to survive in the ministry, I had learned to stuff my emotions and, like a good solider, press on.

During the retreat we visited the Pecos Benedictine Monastery. As we drove through the front gate, I believe God told me that I would return back to this place sometime in the future. This religious community felt like a safe place to come into and to go out from. The quiet and peaceful atmosphere was like oxygen to my soul. It was here that I was introduced to centering prayer. And I did return a couple of years later to receive training to be a spiritual director.

I had no idea how I had ended up in such a place of self-denial and brokenness. Somehow, through my busyness, I had misplaced God's invitation to let him love me – and now I was in danger of not finishing the race. This retreat was a wakeup call. I'd been asleep, and now I was being awakened.

Upon returning home, I continued to write in my journal and simply take time to rest in God's presence. I began practicing the contemplative practice of centering prayer. Centering prayer seemed to be a more sophisticated approach to simply letting God love me as I rested, similar to what I had practiced a decade earlier. In fact, I now know that this kind of prayer was common in the early church. According to Cynthia Bourgeault, "As early as the sixth century St. Gregory defined *contemplatio* [contemplation] as 'resting in God.'"[2]

Those early monks would liken the posture of contemplative prayer to that of a weaned child in his mother's arms. "I have stilled and quieted my soul; like a weaned child with its mother, like a weaned child is my soul within me" (Psalm 131:2).

I also picked up a copy of *Read, Think, Pray, Live* by Tony Jones. Tony Jones is a Presbyterian theologian and writer. He demystified and simplified the practice of *lectio divina* enough for me to understand it. I began to practice this prayer on my own, early in the mornings. To my surprise, God began to speak to me in deep and profound ways. As I experienced his love for me, I could feel my first love and passion for Christ returning. A month into this practice, I heard the Lord tell me to invite my wife to practice *lectio divina* with me, and so we began practicing this prayer model together.

A few months later, at a Christmas party, I was speaking to a former church member and leader who had left our church years earlier for a liturgical congregation. I was discussing how the practice of contemplative prayer was affecting my life, and he challenged me to adopt a liturgical calendar and a liturgical worship service for the purpose of spiritual formation. I had no inclination to take up his challenge at that time, but was intrigued with the idea of spiritual formation. On my way home, as I was talking to God about the conversation, I was reminded of what I had read years earlier by Dallas Willard:

> We can, through faith and grace, become like Christ by practicing the types of activities he engaged in, by arranging our whole lives around the activities he himself practiced in order to remain constantly at home in fellowship of his Father.[3]

It hit me. Spiritual disciplines are not the mark of a mature Christian. Spiritual disciplines are the means by which we become mature Christians. How did I lose sight of this? I had let spiritual disciplines become just another Christian activity I was supposed to do in order to show God and others how committed I was to my faith. The lights came on: Practices like solitude, centering prayer and *lectio divina* are not ends in themselves. The purpose of these activites is to form me, from the inside out, into the person God has called me to be.

To pursue adopting a more traditional church calendar, a liturgical form of worship, or even contemplative prayer, without a clear view toward spiritual formation, will cause one to come to a dead end. I had seen many friends come to a place where Christianity had lost its vitality. They would realign with a new group, excited again about their faith, only to come to the same dead-end place, now only more discouraged and cynical. For me, the means of spiritual formation was not to be found in a style of worship or church calendar (though

I believe that both of these can be very helpful in the practice of spiritual formation). The focus must not even be on contemplative prayer itself. The focus must always be on being more like Jesus. Contemplative prayer is simply a time-tested means of creating space in a busy life where you can meet with Jesus to be changed by him.

After ten years of coming to the end of myself, I was ready to earnestly dive into the love of God.

I had no idea what waited for me. I had spent a lifetime diminishing my emotional pain, living in denial and simply pressing forward to the next activity. I was grateful that the invitation for intimacy was still being extended. In the wisdom of God, rather than making resting in God and contemplative prayer an appendage to an already busy schedule, I was ready to move it to the center and let everything else flow out of that. To put it another way; intimacy with Christ, not ministry for Christ, was my new center. This has made all the difference in the world.

> Without interior transformation the movement up into God's glory would overwhelm us and the movement out into ministry would destroy us.[4]

SPIRITUAL DISCIPLINES AS A PLACE TO ENCOUNTER JESUS

"Come to me, all you who are weary and burdened, and I will give you rest. Take my yoke upon you and learn from me, for I am gentle and humble in heart, and you will find rest for your souls. For my yoke is easy and my burden is light."
Matthew 11: 28 – 30

In his book, *Prayer*, Richard Foster describes three movements of prayer: the upward movement, the outward movement and the inward movement.[1] Each of these movements connects us with God and his purposes. In this chapter, I am not applying this framework exactly the way Richard Foster does in his book, but simply using the three movements as a framework for discussing spiritual disciplines and contemplative prayer.

Upward movement of prayer
The upward movement connects the worshiper with God and with his love for himself. God loves himself and invites us to join him as he gives glory to himself. The upward movement of prayer includes such things as worship, thanksgiving, serving, praise and adoration. Whether it is traditional hymns or

contemporary worship songs, the upward movement of prayer enables us to step into the activity of God as he worships himself.

Who is the most devout worshiper of God? Who takes the greatest pleasure in exalting the Almighty? God himself.[2]

Outward movement of prayer
The outward movement connects the Christian with God, his power and his heart for others. The outward movement includes things as petitioning, intercession and even ministry prayer, such as praying for the sick, freeing the oppressed and counseling the brokenhearted.

These first two expressions of prayer are well established within the Evangelical and Pentecostal expressions of the church. It is the third movement with which many of us are unfamiliar, and that is the place where we are transformed. Without the inner transformation that the internal movement of prayer provides, our inward life is not healthy enough to sustain outwardly-focused service to others.

Inward movement of prayer
The inward movement connects your inner self (your motives, attitudes, self-concept, etc.) with God. With the outward movement, there is a following of Christ into the world. With the inward movement, we are also following Christ, but we are following him inwardly. The inward movement is not about being self-focused. It is being Christ-focused and creating space in our schedules to hear him speak to us about our inner lives. Contemplative prayer falls into this category. The fruit of the inward movement of prayer is inner transformation. It is here that the promise of the gospel of a changed life is realized.

In order to really know God, I must also know myself. Neither my idealized self nor my adult persona is my true self. Beneath the roles and masks lies a self that only God fully knows. This is the self that Jesus asked me to let him into at the retreat for burned-out pastors. This self is the furnace where true transformation takes place. In the words of David Benner, "You are not simply a sinner; you are a deeply loved sinner."[3] God's love is directed toward us just as we are, as sinners.

Evangelicals and Pentecostals are good at following Christ into the darkness "out there." What is missing is the ability to follow Christ into the darkness of our own lives. The inward movement of prayer is about following Christ as he takes you into the darkness of your own soul.

SPIRITUAL DISCIPLINES AS TOOLS OF TRANSFORMATION

There has been a lot written in the Evangelical world in the last 30 years about spiritual disciplines and how to categorize them.

Foster, in *Celebration of Discipline,* speaks of the inward disciplines of meditation, prayer, fasting and study; the outward disciplines of simplicity, solitude, submission and service; and the corporate disciplines of confession, worship, guidance and celebration.[4]

Willard, in *The Spirit of the Disciplines,* speaks of the disciplines of abstinence and the disciplines of engagement. Disciplines of abstinence are those spiritual disciplines – such as solitude, silence, fasting, frugality, chastity, secrecy and sacrifice – that we choose to embrace in order to deny ourselves of something good for something greater. They also tend to counteract sins of commission, which are those sins we tend to fall into such as gossip, pride, greed, lust, gluttony and laziness. Disciplines of engagement help counterbalance the disciplines of abstinence and help us overcome the sins of omission – the omission of the good activities we are called to do that we crowd out of our lives because of busyness or neglect. The disciplines of engagement include study, worship, celebration, service, prayer, fellowship, confession and submission.[5]

I have chosen to divide the spiritual disciplines as upward disciplines, outward disciplines and inward disciplines. These disciplines bring us into contact with God but each moves us in a different direction. The upward disciplines include worship, bible study, fixed-hour prayer, liturgical prayer and fasting. The outward disciplines include intercession, petitioning, praying for the sick and oppressed, service, confession and fellowship. The inward disciplines include solitude, silence, contemplative prayer and journaling.

The inward disciplines, by nature, are reflective and more inclined to move one toward self-discovery through intimacy with Christ. The upward and outward disciplines also help to transform us into the nature of Christ, but the challenge with these first two movements is that it is too easy to approach them as Christian activities rather than a place to encounter God and self.

For example, let's say that your rotation to work in the church nursery has come around, and you find yourself sitting in the nursery, frustrated that you're missing out on the worship time. You are filled with anger and resentment that it's your turn again to serve in an area of church that you don't really even enjoy. What many of us do is simply, in the name of maturity and responsibility, stuff our frustrations (until we get home) and gut it out.

But if Jesus was sitting in the nursery, his attitude would be totally different. Rather than getting out of this frustrating situation by removing yourself from the nursery rotation or beating yourself up for having such a bad attitude, you can use this as an opportunity to be formed into the nature of Christ. You can ask God why you are frustrated. You can ask him to change your attitude into his attitude. Every act of service can be just another Christian activity, or it can be a place to encounter God and be changed into the likeness of Christ. But, in order for this to happen, you must take the time to reflect on the activity, unpack your emotions and dialogue with God.

Willard says,

> In disciplines we need to be informed and experimental. They are not righteousness, but wisdom. We must be practical with them, and not picky. We must not be "heroic" or think we are earning anything from God. Disciplines for the spiritual life are places in which we meet with Jesus to be taught by him, and he is our guide into how they are best practiced. We should not be overly concerned about how others do them. In a very short time Jesus will lead us into the practice of them that is best for us.[6]

The key statement for me is that spiritual disciplines "are places in which we meet with Jesus to be taught by him." If you just approach them as God's to-do list for you, you will either become proud or discouraged. If you approach them as proof of your commitment – and you simply, like a good soldier, press on – you will burn out. Disciplines for the spiritual life are not only intended to change the world, but to change you as well. Again, spiritual disciplines are a place to encounter Jesus.

In her book *When the Soul Listens,* Jan Johnson observes,

> The effort put forth in a spiritual discipline is not to change behavior, but to connect our inner person's motives and needs with God. The effect of that connection is a change of heart.[7]

SPIRITUAL FORMATION

The Bible promises an easy yoke and a changed life. M. Robert Mulholland Jr., of Asbury Seminary, defines spiritual formation as: "a process of being conformed to the image of Christ for the sake of others."[8] I want to take a few moments to comment on his definition, because it is within the context of spiritual formation that contemplative prayer finds it place in the life of a Christian.

Spiritual formation is a process...

Spiritual formation is the process by which people are changed from the inside out. We are all the result of being formed from the inside out. Much of our forming has come from our family of origin and culture. Experiences along the way also help shape us. Some of our formation has been intentional, much of it has happened in our response to life.

Spiritual formation is always a process. Our modern culture likes immediate results. A diet pill is much more attractive than working out at the gym. Putting things on a credit card is faster than saving money to purchase what we want. We find ourselves looking for the next big thing, whether it's the next book, next conference, the next new thing that God is going to do, or the next revival to change us. All these things may be helpful, but it does not discount the fact that true spiritual formation is always a process, and processes always take time. Experiences with God are beneficial in moving us toward maturity, but they do not negate the fact that spiritual formation is a process.

Even experiences with God need to be processed and reflected on for them to have a meaningful and long-term benefit. In our consumer Christian society, we can collect spiritual experiences the same way that compulsive shoppers collect material possessions. One encounter with God that is understood, processed and integrated into our lives is much more helpful than hundreds of spiritual experiences with little thought given to understanding what God might be saying or doing.

...of being conformed...
Christian spirituality teaches us that we cannot form ourselves into the people God has called us to be. Only God can do the forming. Spiritual formation is a work of grace. Information, experiences, good intentions and even spiritual disciplines don't transform us. Spiritual disciplines create a space in our lives where we can partner with God as he changes us from the inside out. Spiritual disciplines do not change us, God changes us.

You can do some things to aid the transformation process, but you do not control it. As Mulholland notes, we live in a do-it-yourself culture, and this aspect of spiritual formation runs against our grain. Being conformed, rather than doing the conforming ourselves, deals with our hesitancy to fully yield control to God and trust him. Being conformed involves surrendering our lives and letting God be in the driver's seat. The good news is that God is a great driver.

...into the image of Christ...
Rather than simply doing Christian activity, we become Christ-like. We become kinder, more patient, more truthful – not because we try harder, but because this is who we are. One of God's greatest gifts to us is to form our character and inner life into the likeness of Christ. In the process of becoming more Christ-like, our false personas get exposed and dismantled so we can become more authentic and true.

Mulholland points out that,

> If, indeed, the work of God's formation in us is the process of conforming us to the image of Christ, obviously it's going to take place at the points where we are not yet conformed to that image. This means that one of the first dynamics of holistic spiritual formation will be confrontation. ... The Spirit of God may probe some area in which we are not conformed to the image of Christ. That probing will probably always be confrontational, and it will always be a challenge and a call to us in our brokenness to come out of the brokenness into wholeness in Christ.[9]

...for the sake of others.
God takes us inward for the purpose of changing us and pointing us outward again. Christ-centered contemplative prayer will always take you inward and back outward.

Concerning this part of the definition, Mulholland writes,

> If we forget this, if we short-circuit our definition, ... we don't have Christian spiritual formation, we don't have holistic spiritual formation. What we have is some kind of pathological formation that is very privatized and individualized, a spiritualized form of self-actualization.[10]

SO HOW DOES CONTEMPLATIVE PRAYER FIT IN TO THE SPIRITUAL DISCIPLINES?

Contemplative prayer is at the heart of the inward disciplines. It is modeled after the relationship that Jesus had with his heavenly Father in the Gospels. It is about simply being with God. It is resting in God as he rests in you. It is consciously being with the one who loves you perfectly. Contemplative prayer is learning to enjoy God as he enjoys you. It involves living in the present moment with God. It is being with God as an end in itself.

Thelma Hall writes,

> Contemplation is a strange new land ... where we learn a new language (silence), a new way of being (not to *do* but simply to *be*), where our thoughts and concepts, our imagination, senses and feelings are abandoned for faith in what is unseen and unfelt, where God's seeming absence (to our senses) *is* his presence, and his silence (to our ordinary perception) *is* his speech. ... To know our true selves is to know we are loved by God beyond all measure.[11]

SUMMARY
God's greatest gift to us is the gift of salvation. To live eternally with an all powerful God who loves us unconditionally is beyond what any of us deserve. To have our inner lives, our interior motives and attitudes changed to that of Christ is to live the abundant life he has promised us.

SPIRITUAL DISCIPLINES AS A PLACE TO ENCOUNTER OURSELVES

"Search me, O God, and know my heart; test me and know my anxious thoughts. See if there is any offensive way in me, and lead me in the way everlasting."
Psalm 139:23, 24

The Johari Window is a psychological tool created in 1955 by Joseph Luft and Harry Ingham. It is used by counselors and personnel managers in the workplace, but it is also a useful tool to help us understand how the power of the gospel can change us from the inside out.

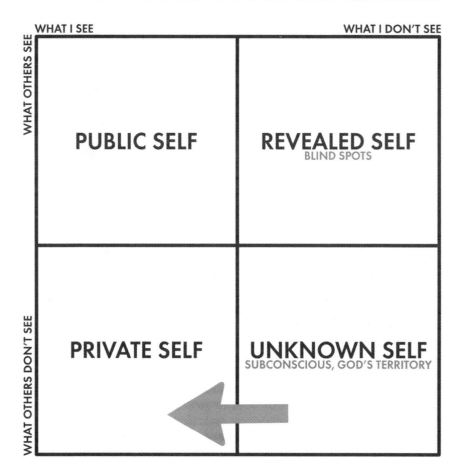

01 Public Self

The first quadrant represents the part of you that you and others see. This is sometimes called the public self. This is that part of our identity that we present to the world. It can be part of our true identity or simply a mask we wear to cover up who we really are. It can be an identity that we have chosen for ourselves or one that has been given to us by others. Many times it is a combination of both. This is sometimes referred to as a persona.

Many times Christians feel pressure to be more than who they really are. We can spend a great deal of time and energy pretending. We feel the pressure to be the competent worker, the loving wife or husband, the perfect parent, etc. We use expressions like, "Never let them see you sweat," "Big boys don't cry," and "Fake it 'til you make it," to prop up the persona we are hiding behind.

In time, we can feel like the wizard from the *The Wizard of Oz,* pulling the levers and declaring, "I am the great Oz," while all along we are simply an inadequate person behind a curtain.

02 Private Self

The second quadrant represents the part of us that we know, but we keep hidden from the world. We all have a private self that we keep to ourselves. Our private self can be private for a number of reasons, some healthy, some not. Some of the healthy reasons are that we all have parts of ourselves that are not appropriate to share with others. For example, a parent needs to wear the persona of a competent caregiver to their small children, regardless of whether they are having a bad day or not. It is never appropriate to share your darkest brokenness with a young child, but it is appropriate to share those kinds of things with a trusted, mature friend or a competent counselor.

The size of our public and private selves changes, depending on the audience. Between my wife and me, my private quadrant is quite small; we try to keep as few secrets from each other as possible. In that sense, in my marriage, my public self is quite large while my private self is quite small, though there still is a private self!

When your public self is a mask constructed to hide a dishonest or deceitful private self, then you are in trouble. When there becomes a real dissonance between your public self and private self, you need to pay attention. This is not healthy.

You need to be careful of the kind of spirituality that encourages you to ignore your private self and simply "fake it 'til you make it." To reduce Christianity to putting on a good public self while ignoring the private self is a real disservice to Christ, others and yourself. In time, the weight of trying to be something in public that you are not in private will do damage to your soul.

We all have a private side that we keep to ourselves and a few trusted friends. Even Jesus only let a few trusted friends join him in the garden before his death (Matthew 26). It was there that it says that he was deeply distressed and troubled. He cried out in the hearing of his friends, "My soul is overwhelmed with sorrow to the point of death." In essence, Jesus was saying that he was so troubled that he wanted to die. He asked God to do the unmentionable: "May this cup be taken from me. Yet not as I will, but as you will." Let us not forget the first part of the prayer. Jesus, in the privacy of the garden and in the company of his closest friends, reveals a side of himself that few had ever seen.

We all have a private self that needs to be nourished. We are not simply actors on the stage of life, we are sons and daughters created in the image of God. In order to become authentic individuals, our public life is a natural expression and outflow of our internal life.

03 Revealed Self

The third quadrant is our revealed self. This is what others see about us, but we remain unaware of. This quadrant contains what are sometimes referred to as our "blind spots." An example is if I am eating at a restaurant and I have unknowingly gotten some food on my face. This information is part of my revealed self – others can see it but I cannot. If you tell me that I have something on my face, then this moves to the public self.

Others always see things about us, both good and bad, that we do not see about ourselves. Whether it's within our family, work associates, social network or church, we need people who love us enough to speak the truth about what they see. Christian community at its best provides a mixture of positive affirmation and loving confrontation. We all have "blind spots," and we need our Christian brothers and sisters, and spiritual fathers and mothers, to speak the truth in love.

04 Unknown Self

The fourth quadrant is our unknown self. This mysterious area is unknown to us as well as to others. It is not unknown to God. He knows us better than we know ourselves, and he continues to love us. In this area we find unknown motives, areas of brokenness, and repressed and forgotten memories. But it is here that our true self lies hidden in Christ.

Our persona strives to put together an identity from secondary things such as success, status, money, family, health and reputation. Our true identity is never found in something we accomplish or earn. It is a gift we receive from Jesus. We are more than our failures and successes. Through taking the inward journey with Christ, we move past our defects and sins, and we find ourselves in him.

In *The Gift of Being Yourself,* David Benner makes this observation:

> Powerful conditioning in childhood encourages us to acknowledge only the most acceptable parts of our self. And parts of self that are not given a place at the family table become stronger, not weaker. Operating out of sight and beyond awareness, they have increasing influence on our behavior.

> Christian spirituality involves acknowledging all our part-selves, exposing them to God's love and letting him weave them into a new person he is making. To do this, we must be willing to welcome these ignored parts as full members of the family of self, giving them space at the family table and slowly allowing them to be softened and healed by love and integrated into the whole person we are becoming.[1]

CHAPTER 3

SPIRITUAL FORMATION AND THE JOHARI WINDOW

Too much of our present spirituality focuses on maintaining our persona for the public self. Those who seek to be authentic followers of Christ take their private selves and public lives seriously. My question is where is the power of the gospel to bring about real transformation? How does the power of the gospel bring its light and transforming power into that part of us we are not cognitively aware of?

Classical Christian spirituality speaks of three or four basic stages every Christian goes through: awakening, purgation, illumination and union. Jesus is intimately involved with us in each of these stages of our growth, changing us into his likeness.

Awakening

Briefly, awakening speaks of that initial "first love experience" that the new Christian walks in on the front end of their relationship with Christ. We encounter God and, many times, ourselves for the first time. This awakening can be gradual or come suddenly. It can come to us at a moment of conversion or as a long process of learning to trust God. We return to this awakening experience many times throughout our relationship with God. There is a sense that we are "awakening" for the rest of our lives. We discover that, in time, we uncover new layers of our knowledge of God and of ourselves.

Purgation

The second stage, purgation, is the purging of those habits, attitudes and actions that are contrary to the witness of the Scriptures and the nature of God. There is a growing awareness of our individual sins and our sin nature. On the front end of our history with God, God deals with the more obvious sins; in time, we discover that he begins to address our attitudes and motives. God invites us to join him as he dismantles the interior structures of our soul that are harmful to us and counter to the Kingdom of God. Many of these structures are inner defense systems we have adopted to survive in a fallen world. We develop patterns of thinking and relating to others that end up doing damage to our souls and to those around us. We develop these patterns long before we learn how to go to God with our pain and disappointments.

We are not cognitively aware of why we do what we do, and others can only guess. We need to create a space in our lives where God can take us into these areas and replace them with the nature of Christ. To walk through this fire of being liberated from our manipulative and harmful internal support systems is not to die but to be transformed and purged.

James Finley, speaking of this process in his book, *Merton's Palace of Nowhere,* writes,

Prayer unveils our heart, allowing it to be cut by God's delicate touch. There is no growth in prayer without some degree of exposure to this purification process out of which the true self emerges in its unexpected splendor.[2]

Here's an example of how this might look: A number of years ago, I was having lunch with an elder and close friend of the church that I pastored. In a moment of real honesty and vulnerability, he shared how he felt manipulated by me. It was not any one thing I said or did; it was a general sense of manipulation he felt from me. Rather than argue or demand proof, I tried to listen deeply because I knew he was picking up on something that others had tried to address as well. He felt the manipulation, and I was becoming aware of it. But as for the root cause, I was totally at a loss.

A few years later, while mediating on Psalm 23, God began to speak to me about my fear of being abandoned. Out of this fear, I sought to control how others perceived me, and in so many subtle ways, I had learned how to tell half-truths and live in shades of gray. He began to show me the many relationships I was manipulating so I could feel safe. He also began to show me how I created a social structure around my brokenness so I could feel I was in control.

This revelation and insight from God was extremely painful and humiliating. And making the necessary changes, both inwardly and socially, though grace-filled, has been extremely challenging. To begin with, I had to face my fears of abandonment straight on. I am still continuing to process this.

Illumination
Illumination is the classical Christian term used to describe the deepening connection we experience with God. It is characterized by a radical shift in our relationship with God. We begin to live a life of prayer. We learn to find God in our pain, as well as in our joy. On the front end of our relationship with God, he is seen as "out there," and, to use a popular contemporary theme, that we are "God chasers." In this season of illumination, we begin to know God in a much deeper and more personal way.

Following seasons of deep purgation, when our interior life is rearranged, we begin to experience the reality of God deep within our being. At this point, we begin to experience in a new way that God, not us, is in control of our relationship. This shift brings a tremendous amount of peace and joy.

Union
Union is the term used to describe our abiding experience of oneness with God. This is sometimes referred to as "spiritual marriage" or "mystical union." This

is a quiet place where we are one in purpose and in character with Christ. In the words of the apostle Peter, we begin to "participate in the divine nature" of God (2 Peter 1:4). All need for human approval or success is surrendered to Christ. This union can be both joyful and painful as we begin to experience God's emotions.

SUMMARY
Through the Johari Window, we see that we have a deep need to understand ourselves, to be changed by God and to walk in the fullness of our identity in him. Thomas Merton defines a saint as "someone who is himself."[3] That "someone" is only found in Christ. The courage to be ourselves comes from our security in God's love.

We never discover that saint on our own; it is only in an honest conversation with God that our false self gets stripped away, and like a butterfly emerging from its cocoon, our true self, created in the image of God, comes forth. In this process of transformation, we discover parts of ourselves that are meant to be explored and brought to life – the artist, writer, dancer, poet or explorer who is also living inside of us.

OUR SPIRITUAL JOURNEY: CULTIVATING AN INNER LIFE THAT SUSTAINS OUTWARDLY-FOCUSED LIVING

"When I was a child, I talked like a child, I thought like a child, I reasoned like a child. When I became a man, I put childish ways behind me."
1 Corinthians 13:11

Throughout church history, people have written about the phases or seasons of our Christian movement toward maturity. In *The Critical Journey: Stages in the Life of Faith,* Janet Hagberg and Robert Guelich capture the wisdom of the church and the insights that Scripture gives us.[1] They provide an integrated, contemporary model for the journey towards spiritual maturity. I have adopted their model, along with insights from Dr. Bruce Demarest (*Soul Guide*)[2], Peter Scazzero (*Emotionally Healthy Spirituality*)[3], Sue Monk Kidd (*When the Heart Waits*)[4], and M. Robert Mulholland, Jr. (*Invitation to a Journey*).[5]

My intention is to provide a framework or context for the process God might be taking you through. This is not to be seen as a detailed road map or a one-size-fits-all kind of spirituality. It is simply one of the ways to describe the journey that all of us are taking. Experience and Scripture teach us that Christian growth is a process. God is always encouraging us and pushing us to grow, but we have the ability to resist him. It takes effort to grow spiritually toward holiness and maturity in a fallen world. Biblical spirituality is always a combination of divine energy and our active participation.

The stages of this journey are progressive and all are necessary – you can't skip one completely. However, this is simply a pattern that many, but not all, people go through in their spiritual lives. These stages are not linear or compartmentalized. You can't finish one and check it off forever. We move at different rates through the stages, and we may even regress, cycle through or get stuck at a stage. Some of us may experience a number of stages at the same time, but most people tend to have a home stage that they are presently living in.

Many like to see the parts of this journey more as seasons than stages. We don't control seasons. We learn to adjust and then thrive and even enjoy the season we are in.

01 First Love
Our journey begins with conversion. This is our starting line. We have an encounter with the love of God, which can be either a gradual or radical experience. Spiritual awakening is a two-sided experience. It is an encounter with the living God; it is also an encounter with our true self.

At this stage, we experience the joy of salvation and, at the same time, may feel weak and unworthy. We can begin to experience purgation for the first time. Purgation is the name of the process that God takes us through as he purges the un-Christlikeness from us. Purgation at this stage involves God speaking to us about sinful actions and lifestyles.

Healthy spirituality is expressed by heartfelt repentance and faith in the character of God. Spiritual disciplines that are helpful at this stage include Bible reading, confession of sin, and corporate and personal worship.

There are people who get stuck at this stage. Sometimes there is an incomplete repentance or an unwillingness or inability to leave an unchristian lifestyle. There are others who never really grasp the reality of forgiveness and spend the rest of their lives struggling with feelings of unworthiness. Still there are others who, because of emotional wounding or addictions, never seem to get very far past the starting line.

To move forward to the next stage, it is important that you find a spiritual family. God will bring you back to this stage many times in your spiritual journey to renew and refresh you.

02 Learning And Belonging

It is important that we, as new believers, get integrated into a local church if we are to grow into maturity. Bible study and Christian community are very important at this stage. In this season, we are eager to learn more about God, the Bible and how to live the Christian life. Many times, we are attracted to strong "black-and-white" leaders who give easy answers to life's problems. We are told that speaking in tongues, Scripture memorization, positive faith, submission to authority or soul-winning is the exclusive key to spiritual growth.

We get stuck at this stage by becoming extremely rigid in our convictions and critical of others. As we emulate our leaders, we often can cultivate an "us-against-them" mentality: conservatives versus liberals, home school versus public school, Evangelical versus charismatic. In our mistrust of other groups, we can form an unhealthy codependent relationship with our own church and its leadership. We can also find ourselves as always the student and never the teacher.

Others of us will find leaders and churches that will encourage us to think for ourselves and challenge us to wrestle with the paradoxes of faith. Healthy spirituality is expressed by a teachable spirit, learning and obeying the truth, active participation in a local church and humility. The spiritual disciplines that are helpful at this stage are Bible study, corporative and personal worship, friendship evangelism, and submission to church leadership. An introduction to contemplative prayer will prove to help center you as a young disciple and help you move toward a more heartfelt and mature faith.

To move forward to the next stage, it is important that you begin serving.

03 Serving

This is described as the doing stage. At this stage, we discover our spiritual gifts and are ready to use our talents to serve. We are ready to roll up our sleeves and get busy. We begin to get active, working for God, serving him and his church. We are becoming responsible and contributing members of the family of God.

The focus of our spirituality and faith is serving God and others. We are praised by the church for our faithfulness and willingness to lay down our lives. The emphasis can be on outward things, such as success through converts, growth in our programs and the good we are accomplishing in our community.

The spiritual disciplines that mark this stage are active church participation, generous stewardship of our resources, courageous serving of others and the faithful use of our spiritual gifts and talents. Some of us may begin stepping into leadership roles at this time. It is essential that we also add a reflective element into our spirituality. We must study the Bible, but not only for the purpose of teaching others; we need to read the Bible for our own spiritual growth. We need to attend a small group that we are not leading. We must search for safe relationships where we can be transparent and accountable. We need to actively set aside times for solitude and restoration. We need to be attentive to the cries of our family for more of our attention. If your family feels that they are competing with God or his church for your time and affection, you will reap a bitter harvest later. We need to be attentive to our own bodies and souls. Are we running on adrenaline? Do we find ourselves compulsively eating, or drifting towards immoral or unwise activities?

Healthy spirituality in this season is characterized by a balance of activity and rest. The challenge is to follow Jesus' example of ministry followed by times of solitude. Having a social life outside of church responsibilities and ministry is a must. It is a good idea to seek out mature Christians or a counselor if your life seems to be out of balance.

We can get stuck at this stage when we simply focus on serving and lose our personal connection with God or ignore our need for rest and restoration. This can leave us feeling empty, resentful and exhausted. It's at this point that we usually "hit the wall."

Crisis
Between stages three and four, there is usually a crisis. This is sometimes referred to as "hitting the wall." The crisis can be precipitated by a natural development, such as a midlife transition; an external event, such as a loss of a job or family problems; or a personal condition, such as burnout or a serious illness. For some, this experience will be simply a midlife transition, while, for others, it will look more like a midlife crisis. The bottom line is that, in this time, we come face to face with our own inadequacy. Our Christian faith as we presently understand it no longer seems to work. This crisis has also been called "the dark night of the soul."

According to many authors, much of the American church is stuck at stage three and never gets past the wall. In order to move forward, we must learn how to move inward. But it takes a tremendous amount of emotional energy to do the inner work that God requires. It may call for temporarily pulling away from stage three activities in order to create the space and the energy to do the inner work.

Many, if not most, of us do not know how to move forward when we've hit the wall. Activity and productivity are such a part of our culture that withdrawing from busyness and going inward seems to be counter-culture and counter-intuitive. So some of us will choose to gut it out and simply serve because this is what we feel is expected from us. Some will simply return to stage one or two, get refreshed, re-tooled, re-envisioned and return to stage three, ready to serve.

27

Others beginning the journey inward are not ready to enter the pain of inner work or to surrender control fully over to God, so they remain at stage three. Others may start the process, feel too alone, confused and afraid, and return to what they are familiar with. Others, because of exhaustion, frustration or disappointments, simply drop out of church. If they don't drop out physically, they do it emotionally. They become warm bodies on the pew.

It is not unusual for people to cycle through these first three stages a number of times before they are ready for stage four. And, sometimes, when returning to stage one or two, people will seek out another church or expression of their faith. They often do this because they feel let down by the previous one or feel that they need new truths, insights or ministry experience to continue growing.

The problem with getting stuck at this point in the journey is that we can think that this is all there is to the faith and never experience the deep work of God in our lives. One of the reasons that people simply cycle is that the church does not know how to help people transition from stage three to stage four. To move forward is a work of grace.

Not everyone's experience with this time of crisis is the same. For those who have learned to process their lives, unpack their disappointments and adjust their expectations in a healthy way, this time will be less traumatic. I believe that if we can teach people, especially leaders in the first three stages, how to develop a contemplative lifestyle, they will go into stage four a lot healthier and better equipped.

Transitioning Into Stage Four
In the next three stages, God begins dealing with the deep-seated structures of our being and behavior. This is the continuation of the purgation process that God began in the first stage. God invites us to cooperate with him in the process of dismantling the false identities and personas we have built for ourselves. God initiates an intense internal restructuring.

Mulholland writes that God begins dealing

> with the deep-seated attitudes and inner orientations of our being out of which our behavior patterns flow. Here purgation deals essentially with our 'trust structures,' especially those deep inner postures of our being that do not rely on God but on self for our well-being.[6]

Sue Monk Kidd, speaking of these "trust structures," writes,

> As we attempt to adapt to and protect ourselves from the wounds and realities of life, we each create a unique variety of defense structures –

patterns of thinking, behaving, and relating designed to protect the ego. *These egocentric patterns make up our false selves.*[7]

Those who can work through this phase are liberated from dependency on manipulative and harmful internal support systems. To walk through this fire is not to die, but to be transformed and purged. Kidd, again writing about her own journey, speaks about the dark night of the soul:

> "There comes a time when both body and soul enter into such a vast darkness that one loses light," wrote Mechtild of Magdeburg. There comes a time when the soul "sinks down into the night."

> John of the Cross … explained that a person may suffer a feeling of abandonment by God, as well as dryness, emptiness, and a distressing encounter with her own hunger. … The purpose of the dark night is to purge us.

> Previous ways of thinking about and relating to God no longer suffice. … Merton tells us that the darkness comes when we allow God to strip away the false selves and make us into the persons we're meant to be. Transformation depends on this stripping away, … a process that involves undoing ego patterns, recasting the old story we created for ourselves to live in, and unraveling illusions not only about ourselves but about God. This stripping away both demands and creates a temporary darkness.[8]

Dr. Bruce Demarest describes the experience of Teresa of Avila, a 16th-century Spanish mystic and reformer in the Catholic Church:

> Teresa of Avila experienced the dark night [of the soul] in a period of intense opposition and suffering. She prayed to the Lord, "Why do you treat me so harshly?" God responded, "This is how I treat all my friends." Teresa replied, "I understand now why you have so few!"[9]

04 Surrendering To The Love Of God
The journey turns inward at this stage. As we've discovered, it is almost always precipitated by and occurring during a time of crisis. For some, the journey inward leads to a crisis, for others the crisis compels them to go inward.

At stage four, we are looking for inner meaning rather than simplistic answers. We may have to pull away from Christian activity for a season while seeking God in a more intimate and personal way. This may be met with confusion and frustration from the church because people, unless they have worked through this stage themselves, have a hard time understanding why you seem to be questioning the faith and are not more active in serving.

God is initiating a stripping away of old patterns of relating to him, to self and to others. This process can be very painful, confusing and draining. It takes much emotional energy to do the inner work God is requiring. The energy that went into keeping up your persona and your false self must now go into doing inner work.

To grow in this stage, we must learn to surrender to the Lord and trust him again. God is doing the restructuring of our inner lives. Our part is to listen, trust, respond and obey. Our goal is to surrender and learn to rest in his love as his beloved child.

This can be difficult because we are in a kind of spiritual darkness, and we are not sure where all of this is going to take us. We can get stuck in this stage by going inward, getting self-absorbed and never coming out. But the inward journey is never about being self-focused. It is about being Christ-centered and learning to follow Christ inwardly. Other people, finding little help in the Christian circles they move in, will look outside of orthodox Christianity and find non-biblical models that are not Christ-centered. There is also the danger of withdrawing from congregational life because it now feels dry, and you may find little support there for this season of your life.

Often we need guidance from a spiritual director or a Christian counselor who understands how God shapes our souls. At the very least, we need someone who has walked this road ahead of us to help us stay on course. It is also helpful to read about the journey of others. There are a number of contemporary Christian authors who have written about this kind of process.

Healthy spirituality in this season is characterized by coming to a mature faith and a radical trust in God. The nature of our relationship with God begins to change. As this happens, there is a decline of anxiety and an increase of faith. We begin to experience what classical Christianity traditionally calls detachment – a posture of actively turning our whole being to God so that his presence, purposes and power can be released through us.

We also begin to experience what historical Christian spirituality refers to as illumination – the classical term used to describe the deepening relationship the Christian experiences with God. Mulholland writes,

> Illumination is characterized by a radical shift of the deep dynamics of our being, a profound transformation of our relationship with God. Illumination is the experience of total consecration to God in love. Rather than my being in charge of my relationship with God, God is given absolute control of the relationship. ...

... The basic shift in illumination is from seeing God as "out there" to an experience of God present deep within our being. This goes hand in hand with the deep level of absolute trust to which the purgative stage brings us. As long as God is perceived as "out there," separated from us, we understand ourselves as independent, autonomous beings. We labor under the anxiety that causes us to attempt to retain control of our relationship with God and to control our limited world.[10]

The spiritual disciplines that are necessary at this stage are those of a contemplative and reflective nature, such as those that we'll explore in the following chapters – the examen, *lectio divina*, times of solitude and sabbaticals. Read how others are processing their journeys. Find a spiritual director or form a spiritual formation small group.

05 Convergence

After the transforming inward journey is launched, Christ directs us outward again. We reconnect with the active world with a new sense of purpose. All true spiritual formation takes us inward and then points us outward again.

Solitude and reflection need to be alternated with times of outwardly-focused activity. It is important that you learn to connect with God in the ordinary events of life. Jesus' life was marked by both solitude and outwardly-focused ministry.

Stage five can look like stage three, but the difference is not so much in our outer activity, but rather in our inner motivation. We may do some of the same activity we did before, we may continue to give leadership and help others, but now we serve out of a new, grounded center. Our spiritually is characterized by less frantic activity and compulsiveness. There is a deep, inner stillness that we have learned to live out of. We have learned to rest even as we work.

For many of us, this is the point of convergence where our giftings, experiences and opportunities converge and we are brought into a season of extreme fruitfulness. Because many of the wrong motivations for fame and recognition have been worked out of us, there is very little inclination toward self-promotion. Some will find the courage to walk away from careers that do not really fit them and come into a more suitable or rewarding line of work. Often a mentor, life coach, spiritual director or counselor is very helpful in helping you find out where you are gifted and called to serve.

There is really no way to get stuck at stage five or six. By this point, we are well on our way toward wholeness and fruitfulness.

06 Integration

We are being transformed by the love of God. Here, we sense in a more profound way God's call to lay down our lives for others. Filled with his love, we are ready to love others selflessly. We worry little about reputation, personal success and comfort. We can love the unlovely, be kind to the rude and pray for our enemies. People are attracted to us because they sense our authenticity. Christ is made perfect in our weakness.

In this stage, there is a real integration of the uniqueness of your personality with the nature of Christ. Your will, character, mission and values are the same as Christ's. You are living the life Christ would live, if he were living your life. You are not perfect. You are well aware of your sin. But you have discovered that his strength is made perfect in your weakness. This union can be both painful and joyful at the same time. At this stage we are living in Christian maturity.

SUMMARY

I have found most churches build a kind of culture around the first three stages. There are congregations that seem to center their home stage around bringing people into the conversion experience, others focus on church as a classroom, and still others are very intent on equipping people to serve. As a pastor, I understood how to move people through these first three stages, but when they hit the wall and were faced with the need to do inner work, the best I could do was to encourage them to "do business with God" (in essence, to cycle again) or refer them to a Christian counselor. I had no understanding of how to help people transition from stage three to stage four.

The first three stages are necessary. There are a tremendous amount of resources for churches to help move their people through these seasons. What is needed is to build within our congregations permission for people to withdraw from activity and then teach them how to create a place in their lives for God to do the inner work that is required for them to move toward emotional and spiritual health. We can equip them with the contemplative prayer models that will help them to grow and thrive in this new season of their lives.

ANCIENT PATHS TO CHRISTIAN SPIRITUALITY

CONTEMPLATIVE PRAYER AS A PLACE

"One day Jesus was praying in a certain place."
Luke 11:1

Contemplative prayer is a place of intimacy.
In the first few centuries following the death and resurrection of Christ, thousands of Christ-followers were led into the deserts of Egypt, Palestine, Syria and Turkey. These disciples came to be known as the Desert Fathers and Mothers. Many lived out their lives of prayer in small caves. These caves were usually only large enough for one person and God. Contemplative prayer is a little like these caves. There is only enough room for you and God.

When I began my own journey into contemplative prayer, one of the first things God told me was to put boundaries around my prayer life. He said, *When we get together, why do we always have to talk about ministry?* He then instructed me not to bring my concerns about the church, the world, my marriage or even my family into this prayer closet. He wanted this time to be about us – him and me. This invitation startled me.

There is a time and place to petition God about the things that concern us, but contemplative prayer is like date night in a marriage. Its primary purpose is to deepen the intimacy of God with his beloved. It is the space you create in your schedule for "us time" with God.

Contemplative prayer is a place where God drives the conversation.
One of the greatest gifts we can give anyone is the gift of listening. We have all had the experience of sitting down with someone who does all the talking while we simply nod and smile politely. We intuitively know that they are not interested in anything we have to say, they are only looking for an audience. Recently, in prayer, God spoke to me about the gift of listening. He said that this is a gift that I had learned to give to him. I was humbled and overwhelmed by what seemed to be his appreciation.

Learning to listen and wait for God to speak is a learned skill. It involves learning to be quiet not just on the outside, but on the inside as well. Ecclesiastes 5:1 reads, "Go near to listen rather than to offer the sacrifice of fools." Learning to listen means that we first learn to quiet our own inner dialogue.

As I have learned to wait for God to initiate the conversation, a couple of things have become apparent. First of all, God is much more interesting than I am. He speaks to us in a myriad of ways: through Scripture, his creation, the counsel of others, the audible inner voice, as well as the still small voice. When he initiates the conversation, he speaks his mysteries and wisdom into our hearts.

Secondly, God wants to speak to us about areas and issues we would rather avoid. Many of these conversations have been painful, but the result is always the same – my inner life is being formed into the character of Christ.

A few years back, as I was meditating on Matthew 5:4, "Blessed are those who mourn, for they will be comforted," the Lord spoke to me and told me that I did not mourn. He went on to say that I knew how to deny, pretend and stuff, but I did not mourn. He followed up with a question, *Why don't you mourn?*

This running dialogue with God led me into a season of extreme emotional pain. I had spent much of my life denying and dismissing my sorrow and emotional pain, so God took me to Psalms to teach me how to be honest with my disappointments and failures. He uncovered in me a real fear. If I acknowledged and owned my emotional pain, I would fall into a black hole that I would never be able to climb out of. Up to that time, I had made living in denial an art form. I had survived by holding the pain at bay, but in the process I'd begun to shut down emotionally.

In the book *The Wizard of Oz* by Frank L. Baum, the Tin Man was a woodsman who came under the spell of a witch. He began to dismember his own body, cutting off his own limbs with his ax and replacing the missing pieces with tin. In the end, there was nothing human left – he was a tin man, wishing he had a heart.[1] My own life resembled that of the Tin Man. Because I was unable and unwilling to face my pain, I began to shut down emotionally – until there was little humanity left. I continued to preach, lead and go through the motions, but I was dying on the inside.

God took me to the abyss of my sorrow and went into the darkness with me. I began to express my pain and anger with the honesty and irreligiosity of King David. As I did, I began to feel the depth of the pain that I would usually deny. I soon discovered that Jesus did not say, "Blessed are those who mourn, for I will take away their pain." He promised to comfort us in the midst of our pain. My religious tin is being replaced with humanity.

Contemplative prayer is a place where you can process your life with God. In the first chapter of Genesis, at the end of each day of creation, God declared it was a good day. He did not have to, but it seemed important to him to take the time to process each day. How many of our days seem to run into each other, where our life seems to be nothing but a blur.

We all have a myriad of experiences, expectations, confrontations and requests coming our way each day. Some of these feed our souls and make us stronger; other things weaken us and tear us apart. It is important that we learn how to process both the good and the bad in the presence of God and wait for his grace and insight. There is a way to be with God where he helps us debrief. And in that debriefing, he comforts and empowers us to move forward.

Contemplative prayer is a place of transformation.
There is power in the gospel to change us from the inside out. Contemplative prayer is not for cowards or mystics. Hebrews 4:12 declares that

> the word of God is living and active. Sharper than any double-edged sword, it penetrates even to dividing soul and spirit, joints and marrow; it judges the thoughts and attitudes of the heart.

Through contemplative prayer, we discover that the Word of God is living and active. The Word of God becomes a living and energizing force in our lives as believers. The Spirit-filled Word has a life and purpose all its own. It begins to penetrate the defenses and excuses we have set up to resist change. Attitudes and thought patterns that have kept us in bondage and sin become exposed, and through cooperation and God's power, we begin to dismantle everything not rooted and grounded in the love of Christ.

We pray not to recharge our batteries for the business of getting back to the concerns of daily life, but rather to be transformed by God so that the myths and fictions of our life might fall like broken shackles from our wrists. ...

... Prayer is a death to every identity that does not come from God.[2]

Contemplative prayer is a place of rest.
The early church fathers defined contemplative prayer as simply resting in the love of God. They used the picture of a weaned child simply resting in the arms of his mother. For so many years, my times of prayer were marked by excessive repentance and broken promises to do better in the future. I still repent when God shows me my sin, but rather than promising to do better in the future, I ask God to make me into the kind of person who no longer does the kind of things that do harm to myself and others and bring reproach to his name. I let go of striving and simply rest in his love.

Contemplative prayer lets go of striving and pretending. We learn to be who we are, not who we wish we were or who we think we should be. We learn to be who we are in the presence of God – our sin, our duplicity, our brokenness is no surprise to Him.

Mulholland speaks of the danger of approaching God the same way we approach a vending machine. But rather than inserting the proper coin, we insert "the right technique, the proper method, the perfect program. ... Or we try to create the atmosphere for the 'right' spiritual moment, that 'perfect' setting in which God can touch us."[3] We do this with the anticipation that we will get what we want from God.

I was taught to put time and emotional energy into prayer, with the expectation that I would be rewarded. I put money into the vending machine, and I expected an answer when I pulled the lever. It is not too much different from me being nice to my wife during the day with the expectation of intimacy later that evening. Healthy relationships do not work that way. Contemplative prayer is simply learning to rest in the love of God with no strings attached.

Contemplative prayer is a place of wonder and surprise.
Ephesians 3 speaks of the width, length, height and depth of the love of God. The apostle Paul goes on to declare that God is able to do more than we could ever hope or desire. Contemplative prayer is a way to explore the love that God has for you. Grace is everywhere! Let God surprise you.

I ask him to strengthen you by his Spirit – not a brute strength but a glorious inner strength – that Christ will live in you as you open the door and invite him in. And I ask him that with both feet planted firmly on love, you'll be able to take in with all followers of Jesus the extravagant dimensions of Christ's love. Reach out and experience the breadth! Test its length! Plumb the depths! Rise to the heights! Live full lives, full in the fullness of God. (Ephesians 3:14 – 19, MSG)

CHAPTER 6
DEVELOPING A
SABBATICAL RHYTHM

"So let's not allow ourselves to get fatigued doing good. At the right
time we will harvest a good crop if we don't give up, or quit."
Galatians 6:9, MSG

How many of us find ourselves getting fatigued doing good? We strive to serve
where we are needed, to seek the lost and to care for the broken. We open up our
lives and homes to others. We say no to our needs and wants, while saying yes to
everyone else.

When my wife and I were on an airplane on our way to a retreat, we were on an
open seating airline. We were tired and worn out. We were among the first on
board and found a place in the first row. We sat back, enjoying the small pleasure
of stretching out our legs. A woman about our age came aboard. She hobbled
along on crutches and seemed to be in pain. She looked our direction as if to say
with her eyes, *Can I have your seat?* Dianna and I looked at her, with a smile
that seemed to say, *No way! We have been giving up our good seats all of our
adult lives and we do not have it in us to do it anymore!* She found another seat
within our range of vision and rubbed her hurting leg the rest of the flight. We

had finally come to the place where we had allowed ourselves to get fatigued doing good.

How do we unpack this Scripture? How do we not allow ourselves to get fatigued? For years my approach was to feel guilty for feeling tired and neglect my need for rest and solitude. I would remind myself that there are people who have it much worse than me. I would think of the martyrs who paid with their lives before me and those who are presently suffering for the cause of Christ around the world. I would repent for my selfishness. In the back of my mind, there was the promise that "at the right time I will harvest a good crop if I don't give up, or quit." I would then double my efforts to serve my family, my congregation, the poor and marginalized. I now believe that the only way for this kind of approach to work is to die young.

In time I found myself simply going through the motions. Doing the right things, but with little passion. The word that people would use to describe me was "faithful." As a pastor and Christian leader, I would spend hours talking and praying for people after a service or workshop. As a husband and father, I would seek to be attentive to the needs of my wife and children. I tried to do the right things that were expected of me, but deep down I wanted to sleep – and run away. I would remind myself that there would be plenty of time to rest in heaven. There was the appearance of fire, but those who got close would recognize there was no longer any heat.

In 2004, I heard a friend of mine, Judy Davids, speak of developing a sabbatical rhythm in our lives. Davids is a licensed counselor, an educator, long-term missionary and has worked with burned-out pastors for years. She defined a sabbatical rhythm as setting aside time to pause, pray and play. I took her lecture to heart and began to reorder my life around this idea of making time to pause, pray and play. Much of the material in this chapter finds its origin in Judy Davids' teachings.[1]

Our lives are brimming over with activity. Bruce Demarest observes,

> Some of us live our lives so chock-full that the Lord can't get our attention long enough to make Himself known. Our psyches are so programmed for action and accomplishment that we're unable to hear God speak. The static in our souls is sufficiently loud that the whisper of the Spirit gets drowned out. Our hurrying disease – or urgency addiction – sucks spiritual life out of us and turns us into hollow performance machines.[2]

Demarest writes of our "psyches ... programmed for action and accomplishment." This is the spirit of the age we live in. Many of us feel that if we are not doing something important or useful, then we are wasting time. To be more efficient, we become experts at multitasking. Busyness is not simply something we engage in, it is the lens that we look through, and it is our strongest cultural value. We feel that if we are not busy, we are not important. Many of us have replaced secular activity with Christian activity, secular noise with Christian noise. "The static of our souls" drowns out the voice of God. There is a kind of static, white noise that is always there, always in the background. It is the noise of our inner critic, our list of unfinished projects, regrets about the past, worries about the future that continue to keep our inner lives at a simmer – just a conversation or mistake away from boiling over.

We are turned into "hollow performance machines." We learn to shut down emotionally in order to be more effective. In the end, we become the Tin Man from *The Wizard of Oz,* wishing we had a heart. This is not the abundant life Christ has called us to live.

I want to look at some Old and New Testament scriptures that speak of a kind of rhythm God has called us to. In introducing the idea of a sabbatical rhythm, I am not speaking of which day to take off (Saturday or Sunday), nor do I want to discuss intricacies of Mosaic Law. I am speaking of building a kind of rhythm in our lives that will enable us to not "get fatigued doing good."

Genesis 2:2, 3
By the seventh day God had finished the work he had been doing; so on the seventh day he rested from all his work. And God blessed the seventh day and made it holy, because on it he rested from all the work of creating that he had done.

Did the all-powerful God rest because he was tired? Was he worn out from the task of designing and building so many solar systems? God rested from his work. I don't think he did so because he was exhausted from creating the universe. I believe he rested to enjoy what he created. In fact, as you read the creation story, at the end of each day he takes the time to enjoy the day's work and declares to himself and to whoever might be listening, "It is good."

In Genesis, there is a kind of divine rhythm that God intends us to follow. Work for six days, followed by rest on the seventh. The pattern is work, work, work, work, work, work, rest. Many of us work, work, work, work, work, work, work, work, work, crash! We crash physically, mentally, emotionally, sexually, spiritually and socially.

As Christians we are called to be like God. And like God, we are called to rest from our work.

Exodus 20:8-11
"Remember the Sabbath day by keeping it holy. Six days you shall labor and do all your work, but the seventh day is a Sabbath to the Lord your God. On it you shall not do any work, neither you, nor your son or daughter, nor your manservant or maidservant, nor your animals, nor the alien within your gates. For in six days the Lord made the heavens and the earth, the sea, and all that is in them, but he rested on the seventh day. Therefore the Lord blessed the Sabbath day and made it holy."

Every seventh day, the people of Israel were to stop working for a full twenty-four-hour period. God did not want the work to be delegated to the immigrant or the employee. The whole nation was invited to take the day off. If God did not even want the animals working, how much more does he us to take a Sabbath?

Leonard Doohan writes that

> people who refuse to rest on the Sabbath or reject genuine sabbatical living are those who trust in their own strength rather than God's grace. ... It is only in the sabbatical pause that we can truly open ourselves to appreciate and acknowledge what God has done.[3]

Leviticus 16:29-31
"You must deny yourselves and not do any work – whether native-born or an alien living among you. ... It is a sabbath of rest, and you must deny yourselves; it is a lasting ordinance."

For many of us, our work is our addiction. If we are being swallowed by busyness, perhaps we want to be swallowed. Many of us use our activity to hide from God and from ourselves. As long as we stay busy, we feel important and useful, even anointed, but in the process, we do damage to our bodies, our relationships and our souls. We are called to even deny ourselves of work.

The Sabbath is to be a "sabbath of rest." It is not enough to leave work physically. We must learn to leave it mentally and emotionally. We are hardwired to need rest. We need physical, mental and emotional rest. This is what contemplative prayer teaches us.

Jeremiah 50:6
"My people have been lost sheep; their shepherds have led them astray and caused them to roam on the mountains. They wandered over mountain and hill and forgot their own resting place."

The prophet Jeremiah speaks of the ancient people of God as lost sheep, led astray by false shepherds. The people of God in our day are still wandering like lost sheep. We are wandering from activity to activity, from responsibility to responsibility. We have replaced secular activities with Christian activities. Many of us have forgotten how to rest and are becoming hollow performance machines.

> **Mark 2:27, 28**
> Then he said to them, "The Sabbath was made for man, not man for the Sabbath. So the Son of Man is Lord even of the Sabbath."

The Sabbath was created for us because we need it! The Sabbath is God's gift to us. Jesus is not only Lord of our work week; he is Lord of the Sabbath as well. We are hardwired to work and to rest – and he intends to be Lord of both.

God never intends for us to become hollow performance machines. God is not a workaholic, neither does he intend for us to be. Developing a sabbatical rhythm means setting aside time to pause, pray and play.

PAUSE
Pausing means making time to slow down and rest. Dallas Willard writes,

> Sabbath is first to be achieved in the practice of solitude and silence. … The body *must* be weaned away from its tendencies to always take control, to run the world, to achieve and produce, to attain gratification.[4]

Pausing also gives us the opportunity to "find the dot." Have you ever been in a large shopping mall or along a walking trail, wondering where you are? If you can find a map in the mall or along the trail, you simply look for the dot that has an arrow pointing to it with the words, "You are here." Many of us go through our days without a clear idea where we are. We lose our temper at those closest to us and wonder, "Where did that come from?" We find ourselves struggling with pornography or depression or compulsive eating – not having a clue what kind of pain or disappointments are behind these harmful activities. Pausing means that you take the time to find the dot. Pausing helps us slow down and find out where we are mentally, emotionally, physically, socially, and spiritually.

We must learn to rest mentally. Many of us, when we begin slowing down on the outside, find ourselves barraged by negative thoughts on the inside. How many of us stay up all night worrying or can only slip into sleep with the sound of the television on? Many of us do not know how to pause mentally. We mistake zoning out via video games, excessive television watching, or drugs for pausing mentally. We simply do not know how to pause mentally.

I have found that centering prayer has helped me quiet my busy mind and overly active imagination. Centering prayer is a way of being quiet and fully present before God. Many times when I wake up in the middle of the night being assailed with thoughts of fear and doubt, I quietly bring my troubled mind before God in centering prayer. I find that like a baby being rocked, I can find sleep again in the love of my heavenly Father.

We must pause emotionally. Some of us treat our emotions as financial bills we don't want to open. We think that if we just stuff them somewhere out of sight, we won't have to deal with them. Just as our financial bills don't simply disappear, neither does our emotional baggage go away. Pausing gives me the opportunity to ask myself, "Is my sarcasm really disguised anger? Is my sadness rooted in my frustration with life? Is my compulsive eating really an expression of my feelings of isolation? When I find myself snapping at our children, am I really angry with my spouse or with my job?"

God wants us to pay attention to our emotions and process them honestly in his presence. For many of us there is pain behind the pain, a sin behind the sin that must be faced if we are truly going to be free. As a pastor, the only way I knew how to stay in the ministry was to shut down emotionally. In time, I found myself emotionally distant from my congregation, my staff and my family. Ministry provides enough "open doors" to keep one busy for a number of lifetimes. Christian activity provides many of us the cover we are looking for so that we don't have to take the time to honestly process our daily emotional wounds. Dr. Robert Clinton lists our inability to receive healing for our emotional and psychological wounding as one of the primary reasons seventy percent of pastors don't finish well.[5] What we don't process in private, we will act out in public.

Practicing contemplative prayer helped me to invite God into my emotional pain and find healing for the pain behind the pain. Through leaning into the pain with God, I was able to discern the occasions when my pain was rooted in sin. Through the grace of God, this led to repentance, forgiveness and redemption.

We need to rest physically. Dallas Willard observes that "the body lies right at the center of the spiritual life."[6] The Bible speaks of sin dwelling in our bodies (Romans 7:12-20). Our bodies not only remember how to sin, but they also remember righteousness. I believe that, as Americans, activity must dwell in our bodies. We are programmed for action and busyness. I'm not saying that activity is sinful, but when we lose our ability to slow down, there is something wrong with our spirituality. In order to finish the race that God has called us to, we need to train our bodies for quietness and rest.

Again, Dallas Willard writes,

> If we are not rested ... the body moves to the center of our focus and
> makes its presence *more strongly* felt, and the tendencies of its parts call
> out more strongly for gratification. The sensual desires and ego demands
> will have greater power over us through our desperate body and its parts.
> In addition, our awareness of what it is doing – it is very subtle – and
> what is happening around us will be less sharp and decisive. ... Weariness
> ... can make us seek gratification and energy from food or drugs, or from
> various illicit relationships, or from egoistic postures that are, in Paul's
> words, "upon the earth." They pull us away from reliance upon God and
> from living in his power.[7]

There is a type of energy that we get from sin – an instant gratification. When
our bodies and our minds are tired, we are the most vulnerable. Sin energizes
us in a way that ultimately destroys our souls. But there is divine strength that
comes from quietness and rest. The tragedy is that so few Christians and leaders
know how to find it. Contemplative prayer positions one to receive the strength
that can only come from God.

> "In repentance and rest is your salvation, in quietness and trust is your
> strength, but you would have none of it" (Isaiah 30:15).

The Sabbath is first of all, a Sabbath of rest. And out of that rest we find God's
strength.

PRAY

Prayer is the primary work that is to mark our spiritual lives. Our prayer lives
are to be marked by times of worship, intercession and petitioning. Prayer is one
of the most important activities we are called to do. When speaking of living
within a sabbatical rhythm, I am speaking of prayer as a place rather than an
activity. We need to continue with the work of intercession and petitioning, but
we are to set aside times where we "do no work" and simply rest in the love of
God. Prayer becomes a place we go to and come out from. The focus of this
book is prayer as a place of intimacy, rest and transformation.

Many friends of mine participate in the ancient Christian practice of praying the
Daily Office as a means of pausing and praying during the day. The Daily Office
is also called fixed-hour prayer, Divine Hours or Liturgy of the Hours. The focus
of the Daily Office is not to get something from God, but to be with God and
commune with him all through the day. It involves reading and praying portions
of Scripture and formalized prayers. Jesus and the Jews of his day prayed at set
hours of the day. After Jesus' death and resurrection, his disciples continued to
pray at fixed hours of the day (Acts 3:1; 10:3, 9, 30). This practice has continued
to be an important part of many Christian groups for the last 2000 years.

The important thing to remember is that we need to establish a time and place where we learn to simply rest in God and be with him. Peter Scazzero makes the observation that, "Mother Teresa of Calcutta required her Missionaries of Charity to spend three one-hour blocks of time a day for prayer to sustain their love for the dying."[8]

We may not have to face the intensity of heartbreak and suffering that Mother Teresa and her Missionaries of Charity faced every day. But we all live in a world marked by brokenness and violence. We all suffer at the hands of wounded people with good and bad intentions. We are all faced with problems and challenges that are bigger than us. We all need to find prayer as a place we come to in order to be sustained. We need to come to this place of prayer with no agenda. We are called to rest in God as he rests in us.

PLAY

There is a kind of play we can engage in that restores our soul. Much of what we do for entertainment is simply zoning out. Play and leisure is meant to leave us energized and restored.

Each of us needs to discover how to play in such a way that refreshes our soul. It can be gardening, getting up early on Saturday morning and hitting the yard sales, fishing, having friends over for dinner, reading a good novel or simply taking long walks outdoors.

The thing that separates work from play is not so much the activity itself. Rather, it is the reason you are doing what you are doing. If you are doing it to make a living or for someone else, then it's work. If you are doing it because you enjoy it, then its play. Learning how to play is not as easy as it sounds.

Growing up, I loved to draw. As a child I would draw for hours. Over the years this practice was reduced to doodling on scratch paper while having boring and life-draining conversation over the telephone. A number of years ago, I returned to doing pen-and-ink drawings. When I initially started drawing again, I felt this pressure to do it for others. In other words, I felt this inner drive to draw well so that others would think I was a good artist. Play had become work once again. Through prayer and intense inner work, I was able to return to the place where I draw for myself because I enjoy it and it feeds my soul.

Another way that I play is to take long walks in nature. I know that there are health benefits to regular walking, but I don't walk for those reasons (that would be called exercise). I walk because it feeds my soul and because I enjoy seeing what God has created. It is a divine waste of time.

Our culture pushes us to put a utilitarian value on everything. We approach our friendships, our church affiliation, our relationship to nature and even our play as having value in as much as it contributes to work and helps us to be successful. We used to play tennis, now we "work on our serve."

Play within the context of a sabbatical rhythm is meant to help us slow down, enjoy our life and find rest. We are to find rest not only for our bodies, but for our minds as well. Leland Ryken writes, "Any leisure activity will become just another form of work if pursued with the compulsion of work."[9]

It is up to you to discover how to play in a way that honors God and feeds your soul. What may look like play to me, may be work for you. My friend Brian loves to cook Thai and Indian food. His wife is presently going to college, and he is now doing much of the daily meal preparation for his family. The daily meals are work, but occasionally he invites some close friends over for Thai food, which he loves to cook. This is play for him. Work is what you have to do, play is what you want to do.

God used the contemplative prayer model of the examen (chapter 8), to get me in me touch with my playful self again. I must also confess that I needed to develop a theology for playing so I could play without guilt. I had such a strong and warped work ethic that I had a difficult time making play a priority in my life. Ryken's book *Redeeming the Time: A Christian Approach to Work & Leisure* was really beneficial in helping me find a balance.

PUTTING IT ALL TOGETHER

We are responsible for our own lives. Whether we are a parent, a businessperson or a church leader, we are responsible to learn to live within our profession. In other words, every line of work and responsibility has its own set of challenges, expectations and pressures. It's your responsibility to figure it out how to live within your vocation without burning out. It is your responsibility to set aside the time to slow down and rest. God is waiting to meet you in quietness and prayer, he wants to love and empower you. You are much more than a tool in God's hand, you are his child. God made the world as beautiful as it is for his glory and our enjoyment.

Developing a sabbatical rhythm is a must. Your rhythm will look different than mine. We are at different stages in our lives. We are wired differently. I am an introvert; my wife is an extrovert. Our sabbatical rhythms look different. To ensure I don't burn out again, I have established a daily, weekly, monthly and yearly sabbatical rhythm in my life. My sabbatical rhythm is uniquely mine; I would never want to impose this on anyone else.

My daily sabbatical rhythm involves getting up early before the children wake up, making a cup of coffee and spending some time in contemplative prayer, journaling, and listening to God. It is here where I find the dot. Sometimes I do this alone; sometimes I do it with my wife. (*I am a morning person and she is a night person.*) Later in the day, sometimes at noon or after work, I take a walk in a local park, and I spend some time drawing in my journal. Once a week, I attend Sunday worship service with my family and take an extended time for walking in the park. Once a week, we also gather as an extended family. Our grown children, their children, and our children still living at home gather for a weekly meal together. It is an opportunity to laugh, reconnect and enjoy each other's company. Once a month (but not every month) my wife and I try to go out of town for a long weekend and spend the time together, either alone or with friends. Once a year, I take a week-long contemplative prayer retreat.

We'll discuss how to integrate a contemplative lifestyle into your routine in chapter 12, A Track to Run On. Building a sabbatical rhythm is about building a pattern in your life where you don't burn out, lose your marriage or lose your sense of who you are. God promises that if we don't give up or quit, there will be a rich harvest waiting for us.

"Are you tired? Worn out? Burned out on religion? Come to me. Get away with me and you'll recover your life. I'll show you how to take a real rest. Walk with me and work with me – watch how I do it. Learn the unforced rhythms of grace. I won't lay anything heavy or ill-fitting on you. Keep company with me and you'll learn to live freely and lightly."
(Matthew 11:28-30, MSG)

CENTERING PRAYER: RESTING IN GOD

"My soul waits in silence for God only; from Him is my salvation."
Psalm 62:1, NASB

At first glace, centering prayer looks like something straight out of the New Age movement or the Eastern religions. But centering prayer is distinctively different from Eastern meditation. With those forms of prayer, you attempt to empty your mind of all thoughts. Centering prayer allows for the recognition of thoughts and gently releases them to God. This form of prayer focuses on the awareness of the Holy Spirit residing in the heart of the Christian. The goal of centering prayer is to be attentive to the presence of God within. It is a kind of prayer model few non-Catholic or Orthodox Christians have been exposed to.

This prayer may seem mysterious to some because it depends so little on words. We do not give God information about all our needs, projects, ideas, programs, plans and agendas. We don't suggest things we would like him to do. We sit in the presence of God and give him our undivided love and attention. …

Because centering prayer is a way of being with Jesus that doesn't cover prayer concerns, some people wonder if it counts as real prayer. Furthermore, if it doesn't make you feel or experience something particular, what does it do? ... In centering prayer the goal is to so dwell in Christ that the fruit of this dwelling begins to show up in your life. Centering prayer may "do" nothing at the moment. You sense no rapture, no mystical bliss. But later, as you move out into the busyness of life, you begin to notice that something has shifted. Your quiet center in Christ holds. Centering prayer trusts that being with Jesus brings transformation.[1]

Centering prayer finds its origins with the early Desert Fathers. John Cassian (AD 360-430) was born in what is now Romania. He made a 20-year pilgrimage to the deserts of Egypt to learn about contemplative prayer. Around 415 AD, he moved to the south of Gaul (France) and established a monastery for men and a second one for women. Cassian was deeply impacted by the Desert Fathers and wrote his book, *The Conferences,* about his conversations with many of the contemplatives he had spent time with.

Taking his lesson from the Desert Fathers, Cassian's focus in prayer was that of inner freedom of the soul, listening to God and being conscious of the indwelling presence of God. He encouraged his monks to repeat a simple prayer: "O, God, come to my assistance; O Lord, make haste to help me."[2] The purpose of this prayer was to bring the believer to a place of inner stillness before the Lord. He taught that the believer must achieve a state of silence and contemplation, and then God would work in his heart.

Cassian's approach to contemplative prayer was the primary monastic practice for 10 centuries in the West; he influenced Saint Benedict, among others. It is the fourth stage of *lectio divina.* However, during the Scholastic period (12th - 15th centuries) theologians like Thomas Aquinas recovered the works of Aristotle and other ancient thinkers. Contemplative spirituality began to be discouraged in the church and, in time, was seen as something reserved for the spiritually elite.

In the 14th century, an unknown author in England wrote *The Cloud of Unknowing.* The anonymous author urges the young disciple to move beyond simply thinking about God into a place of utter stillness before God. Here is some of the text within *The Cloud of Unknowing:*

> Center all your attention and desire on him and let this be the sole concern of your mind and heart. ... If you want to gather all your desire into one simple word that the mind can easily retain, choose a short word rather than a long one. ... But choose one that is meaningful to you. Then fix it in your mind so that it will remain there come what may. ... Be careful

in this work and never strain your mind or imagination, for truly you will not succeed in this way. Leave these faculties at peace. ... It is best when this word is wholly interior without a definite thought or actual sound. ... Let this little word represent to you God in all his fullness and nothing less than the fullness of God. Let nothing except God hold sway in your mind and heart. ... No sooner has a person turned toward God in love than through human frailty he finds himself distracted by the remembrance of some created thing or some daily care. But no matter. No harm done; for such a person quickly returns to deep recollection. ... Should some thought go on annoying you, demanding to know what you are doing, answer with this one word alone. If your mind begins to intellectualize over the meaning and connotations of this little word, remind yourself that its value lies in its simplicity. Do this and I assure you these thoughts will vanish.[3]

Modern day writers on centering prayer include Thomas Keating, John Mann, M. Basil Pennington, and Cynthia Bourgeault. Each of these writers has their own variations on how to do centering prayer, but I've adapted this basic formulation from Tony Jones' book *The Sacred Way*[4]:

01
Find a quiet place where you will not be disturbed. Express to God your desire to be with him. Give yourself a few moments to settle down.

02
As you sit comfortably with your eyes closed, let go of all thoughts, tensions and sensations that you may feel, and begin to rest in the love of God who dwells within.

03
Effortlessly, choose a word or short phrase. This is a symbol of your intention to surrender to God's presence, and let the word be gently present within you. The word or phrase should communicate God's love to you. As you find yourself quiet on the inside, feel free to let go of your word or phrase.

04
When you become aware of thoughts or as internal sensations arise, take this as your signal to gently return to the word or phrase, and return to your intention to let go and rest in God's presence.

05
If thoughts subside and you find yourself restfully aware, simply let go of the word or phrase. Just be in the stillness. When thoughts begin to stir

again, gently return to the word or phrase. Use your word or phrase as your only response to thoughts, questions, or anxieties that arise in your mind.

06
At the end of the prayer time (20 minutes in the morning and evening is a good balance), take a couple of minutes to come out of the silence – even if you don't feel you need it. Many people find this a perfect time to internally express to God their thanks and to pray for others in need of God's grace. Slowly reciting the Lord's Prayer is another gentle way to come out of the prayer.

The purpose of centering prayer is not to get a word from God or any sort of divine revelation or experience. My usual phrase is "I receive your love." I then see myself breathing in the love and spirit of God.

Again Jesus said, "Peace be with you! As the Father has sent me, I am sending you." And with that he breathed on them and said, "Receive the Holy Spirit." (John 20:21, 22)

Centering prayer is simply being attentive to the presence of God as he dwells within – resting in him as he rests in you.

THE EXAMEN: PAYING ATTENTION TO GOD

"Finally, brothers, whatever is true, whatever is noble, whatever is right, whatever is pure, whatever is lovely, whatever is admirable – if anything is excellent or praiseworthy – think about such things."
Philippians 4:8

When I enter into a relationship with someone as a spiritual director, I ask them to do the examen for 30 days and to keep a journal of their experience. I do this because God is active in their lives, and I want to help them to pay attention. God is speaking to us in ways that many of us are unaware of. It is as if he is laying out food for your soul every day and you don't know how to find it. Paying attention is a learned skill. We must learn to pay attention to God, to our souls, to our physical bodies, and to others. The examen is a way to learn how to pay attention to God's activity in our lives and hear what he has to say to us about what we recently experienced. It is a kind of debriefing that allows you to process your day with God.

The apostle Paul held the strong conviction that God is active in the lives of those who love him, that God is working in all the events of our lives toward forming our inner lives into the likeness of Christ.

We know that in all things God works for the good of those who love him,
who have been called according to his purpose. *For those God foreknew*
he also predestined to be conformed to the likeness of his Son, that he
might be the firstborn among many brothers. (Romans 8:28, 29, emphasis
mine)

The examen is a way to discern God's activity in both the positive and negative
forces that come our way.

This simple prayer form comes out of the *Spiritual Exercises* of Ignatius Loyola
(1491-1556). This prayer exercise so impacted his own life that he wanted
everyone to be taught how to do the examen. The examen is basically a daily
examination of our deepest feelings and desires. Ignatius called these feelings
our consolations – what connects us with God, others and ourselves – and our
desolations – what disconnects us. He believed that God speaks to us through
our consolations and desolations.

Some of the characteristics of consolations are that they can be encouraging,
strengthening, joyful, satisfying, give inner freedom or a sense of vitality – they
are life-affirming. Some of the characteristics of desolations are that they leave
you feeling discouraged, sad, full of anxiety, trapped or overburdened – they are
life-draining.

The genius of this prayer is that you are not simply looking inwardly. You are
asking God to help you review your day and show you what energized you and
what disempowered you, and then give you his perspective on your consolations
and desolations. This interaction can lead to real transformation.

O LORD, you have searched me and you know me. You know when I
sit and when I rise; you perceive my thoughts from afar. You discern my
going out and my lying down; you are familiar with all my ways. (Psalm
139:1-3)

Once God speaks to you about your consolations and desolations, ask for
discernment. Ask God what is it about the experience or event that caused it
to be a consolation or desolation. Ask him to speak into the consolation or
desolation and give you his insight and wisdom. This second question can lead
into deep inner work. When speaking to him about your desolations, along with
insight, ask for his healing presence and comfort.

The first time I tried this prayer was one evening after my wife and I returned
from a leadership meeting for our church movement. The meeting ended in the

late morning with a tremendous time of worship followed by communion. We checked out of the hotel and headed to the airport. To our surprise, we ran into a national Christian leader and his wife. The four of us had a quick lunch at the airport and then boarded our planes back home. That evening I asked God to show me my consolation. I invited God to help me review my day and show me the point that he poured out his grace and I felt the most energized. I was sure that it would be the meeting we had with the other couple at the airport or perhaps the worship experience that morning. To my surprise, God reminded me of Dianna reaching over and touching my arm on the flight back home. I was reminded of the love and affection I felt as she held onto my arm. To be honest, I had forgotten about this incident a few moments after it happened. Yet when I asked God to show me how he had met me that day – this was my consolation – this was his primary expression of grace being poured into my life.

I lay in bed shocked and surprised how unaware I was of God's intervention in my life. I was surprised that apart from his revelation, I was totally unaware of how God imparted his love and grace to me that day. When I asked God why this was my consolation, he began to speak to me about what a gift from him my wife is to me. He followed that with an admonition to show her much more appreciation and care.

If you practice the examen for an extended period of time, you can begin to see patterns of consolations and desolations. These patterns may be indications of God trying to get your attention about an area of your life or an indication of his will and direction. I try to practice the examen for a 30-day period at least once a year. The first time I did this practice for 30 days in a row, I discovered that every time I took a long walk in a park, that was my consolation. Again, this was a surprise because whenever I took the time to walk alone, I always had to fight feelings of guilt. I struggled with the thoughts that I was wasting time and that I should be doing something more productive. The activity that was giving me life on one hand was at the same time causing me distress. To put it another way, the thing that God was using to give me life, I felt that I did not have permission to pursue. After some prayer and reflection, I made the decision to include walking in solitude as a central component of my spiritual life. If God wanted to feed my soul this way, then I would be foolish not to adjust my daily schedule to his provision.

God also intends to speak to us through our desolations. In fact, I have discovered that as I learned to lean into my pain rather than draw away, this can be a pathway to real inner change. God has much to speak to us about concerning our pain and sinful activities. Many times behind our outbursts of anger, there may be feelings of being treated unfairly; behind our lapses into compulsive eating, there may be deep feelings of isolation. As I have asked God to speak to me about my sinful attitudes and actions, I have discovered that many times there is a sin behind the sin. As I confess my sin and invite God into that part of my life, I find that he comes with forgiveness and redemption.

It is not surprising that many of our desolations may involve people close to us, such as our spouses, children or co-workers. This does not mean that you must get rid of your painful relationships. Rather, ask God to show you what it is about the relationship that makes it a desolation. What is it about this relationship that makes me so angry, so frustrated or so filled with hopelessness? Sometimes God will speak to you about a part of you that must change, other times he simply wants to comfort and empower you to endure. The important thing is to invite God into your desolation and rest in his love for you.

Once, when I was doing a workshop about contemplative prayer, a young woman asked if the goal was to eventually not have any desolations. I replied that this won't happen on this side of heaven. The goal is not to have a pain-free life. The goal is to join with God in your desolations and let him transform you into the image of Christ.

God has used this practice of the examen to show me the many channels he intends to use to empower me with love and grace. He has used it to show me how to play in a way that restores my soul. Through processing my consolations and desolations, he has helped me to bring a greater measure of health to difficult relationships. By paying attention to my consolations and desolations, I have found the courage to embark on a new direction for my life. Through this daily debriefing with God, I was able to make my way through my own midlife crisis.

For those who are hitting the wall or going through a midlife transition, the examen is a very useful prayer model. It takes a great deal of emotional and mental energy to process life changes during a time of transition. But God has insight and strength for you during the dark night of your soul – and the examen helps you find it.

HOW TO PRACTICE THE EXAMEN
The consolation and desolation steps each have three parts. The first involves asking God to help you locate your consolation or desolation. In the second part, you revisit the emotions and allow yourself to experience them again. The third part is called the discernment – you ask God to speak to you concerning your joy or pain.

To begin, find a place where you can relax and be quiet. Acknowledge God's love for you and his involvement in your life.

Step One **Consolations**

01

Ask God to bring to your awareness the moment today for which you are most grateful, which gave you strength, in which you felt the most energized and alive, etc. Sometimes it helps if you go back in your mind to the moment you woke up and then fast-forward through your day. If more than one consolation comes to mind, choose one to focus on.

02

After you locate this moment, step back into it and let yourself relive the joy of that event. (Remember, at the end of each day of creation, God reminded himself that, "It was good.") Thank God for the consolation you experienced. Allow yourself a few moments to enjoy your consolation again, stepping back into the life-giving moments you experienced.

03

Ask God to show you what it was about that event that gave you life. What was said and done that made that moment so life-giving? Sit still and wait for him to respond. If you journal, you might want to write out your dialogue with God. If he does not say anything at this time, simply rest in his love for you.

Step Two **Desolations**

01

Ask God to bring to your awareness the moment today for which you are least grateful, where you experienced sadness, shame, failure or anger, where you felt life and energy being drained from you, etc.

02

After you locate this moment, step back into it and relive the feelings without trying to change or fix it in any way. Let yourself revisit your pain. It is imporant that you are honest with your painful emotions. Many of us have been taught to diminish or make light of our pain. This does not benefit us in the long run; it is much more important to be honest with yourself and God. When I am journaling this exercise, I simply write out what I am feeling, such as, "This makes me so angry, and I feel really humiliated."

03

Ask God what is was about that event that made you so angry, sad, helpless, shameful, etc. Listen to what he has to say. Again, if you journal, you might want to write down your insights and conversation with God.

Ask God to comfort you and fill you with his love, and sit in silence for a few moments.

Step Three Thankfulness
Give thanks for whatever you have experienced during the day. Thank God for being present with you in your consolations and desolations.

This prayer can be practiced alone or with others. Many parents I know practice this prayer with their children as they put them to bed at night. At an early age, they've already begun teaching their children how to process the events of their lives. With younger children, they can ask God to show them what made them glad and what made them sad.

Practicing this prayer will help you make better decisions. It helps you to see patterns in your life. This is why it is so important to record or journal your insights over a period of time.

I have taught this prayer model to thousands of people over the last few years. It never ceases to amaze me how astonished people are when God reveals to them their consolations and desolations. More times than not, people are surprised by the "nonreligious" ways that God empowers them with grace. God loves us and is active in our lives. He has the power and wisdom to take even the most painful event and turn it into a transforming experience.

And we know that in all things God works for the good of those who love him, who have been called according to his purpose. For those God foreknew he also predestined to be conformed to the likeness of his Son. ... (Romans 8:28, 29)

CHAPTER 9

JOURNALING AS A PLACE OF PRAYER AND TRANSFORMATION

"We were under great pressure, far beyond our ability to endure, so that we despaired even of life. Indeed, in our hearts we felt the sentence of death. But this happened that we might not rely on ourselves but on God, who raises the dead."
2 Corinthians 1:8, 9

There are a number of reasons to keep a journal. Stress relief, personal growth, processing and recording events are a few. Journaling is also one of the easiest and most powerful ways to deepen your relationship with God. By getting your thoughts and prayers out of your head and onto paper, you gain insights you would never see otherwise. One of the surprises I discovered was that by inviting God into my practice of journaling, writing became a place of transformation. Adele Calhoun writes:

> In a consumer society it's easy to accumulate experiences, believing the more we have the better! Yet experiences don't necessarily bring wisdom, nor do they automatically transform us. We need to listen and reflect on our experiences in the presence of the Holy Spirit to learn from them. Journaling is a way of paying attention to our lives.[1]

My approach to journaling is an integration of the disciplines of journal writing, with some of the elements of *lectio divina,* centering prayer, and the examen.

My process is:

01

Write out my concerns with as much emotional honesty as I can muster. I call it leaning into the pain. Writing helps me to own my disappointments rather than dismissing or diminishing them. I try to be as honest with myself as possible. In the past I would push my emotional pain away and seek comfort in keeping busy or turn to the refrigerator and then the television for comfort. Or I would be ashamed of how I was feeling, so I would not be honest with my emotional life. Now I lean into my pain in the presence of God.

Concerning facing the parts of ourselves we would rather ignore, David Benner writes:

> To truly know something about yourself, you must accept it. Even things about yourself that you most deeply want to change must first be accepted – even embraced. Self-transformation is always preceded by self-acceptance. And the self that you must accept is the self that you actually and truly are – *before you start your self-improvement projects!*

> Any hope that you can know yourself without accepting the things about you that you wish were not true is an illusion. Reality must be embraced before it can be changed. Our knowing of ourselves will remain superficial until we are willing to accept ourselves as God accepts us – fully and unconditionally, just as we are.[2]

02

Then I turn my concerns into a prayer and write them out. I tell God how much pain I am in and ask him for input, grace and comfort. To lean into your pain and not bring it to God will only lead to more despair. It is important to turn your pain into prayer. Then with an expectant heart, I lean into God again and wait on him.

03

As I am leaning into him, there are times when I sense his love, grace and wisdom. I write out my conversation with God, and then I lean into God again, this time with a grateful heart and rest in his provision. My purpose is that the event I am writing about can be used in the hands of God to transform me into the image of Christ.

Most of the time I don't hear or sense anything at all; if this is the case, I rest in his love (centering prayer) with the faith that he has heard me. I trust that he will empower and enlighten me in his time.

A number of months ago, I was informed by email that I would not be invited back to teach a missions class. I was not told this by the person in charge of bringing in the teachers; the information came to me through the grapevine. Though I was popular with most of the students, the administration felt I was "too charismatic." My feelings were hurt and I was angry. I carried this around for a few days before I sat down to journal my experiences. I went through the steps, but the only thing I received in step three was a sense that I was still looking for identity from secondary sources, those in authority. To be honest, this was not what I was wanting to hear from God. This insight provided no real comfort at the time. But I brought this part of my brokenness to God and asked for his grace to change. A number of months later, as I was going about my business, I heard the Lord speak to me about the incident and rejection I experienced. He said, *It was not a good fit for you and you are not a good fit for them.* With that came a peace about the whole situation.

I get this formula from Psalm 3, from the prayers of Jesus in the garden, and from the life of Paul.

David
In the Psalms, the word "selah" is used to indicate that the reader is to stop to rest and reflect.

> Resting and reflecting on the God encountered in Scripture is encouraged in Psalms and Habakkuk with the word selah, which occurs seventy-four times. Though it is often dismissed as a mere musical notation, most commentators agree that selah was inserted at points where the singer or psalm reader should pause so listeners could reflect.[3]

I read many of the Psalms as a kind of spiritual journal King David kept to process his own struggles. Perhaps before they were made to be part of the worship liturgy of Israel, they were first real struggles that David worked through. Psalm 3 comes out of David's experience of rejection and betrayal by his son Absalom. Absalom had raised an army of thousands of solders and marched into Jerusalem through the front gate as David was fleeing out of the back gate. David's wives were publicly raped and people began to declare that God was no longer with David.

> O Lord, how many are my foes! How many rise up against me! Many are saying of me, "God will not deliver him." Selah (v. 1, 2)

In these first two verses, David expresses that many people had risen up against him and people are beginning to mock him. David, after he escaped from Jerusalem, hid in the caves while Absalom's army looked for him. Rather than gutting it out, David expresses his dilemma in the presence of God. This is followed by "selah" – pausing and reflecting.

Following this same pattern, I write down my own pain and struggles. I express, in writing, the emotions I may be experiencing such as embarrassment, shame, anger, lust, etc. I try to be as specific as possible, i.e. "such-and-such person really hurt me." When I feel that I have honestly gotten in touch with my emotions, I lean into them in the presence of God. Then I am ready to move to the next part of the prayer.

> But you are a shield around me, O Lord; you bestow glory on me and lift up my head. To the Lord I cry aloud, and he answers me from his holy hill. Selah (v. 3, 4)

In verse three, David reminds himself of who God is, and then he cries out to God. Again, this part of his journaling is followed by taking the time to pause and reflect.

Following this pattern, I turn my pain into a prayer. I express in writing what I am feeling and I ask God to meet me in this place of turmoil. Then I put down my pen and rest in his presence. Many times I move into centering prayer as I wait for God.

> I lie down and sleep; I wake again, because the Lord sustains me. I will not fear the tens of thousands drawn up against me on every side. Arise, O Lord! Deliver me, O my God! Strike all my enemies on the jaw; break the teeth of the wicked. From the Lord comes deliverance. May your blessing be on your people. Selah (v. 5-8)

Something really miraculous happens between verses 4 and 5. I am sure that hiding out in a cave while tens of thousands of soldiers are looking for you can be extremely distressing. The natural physical reaction to such stress would be extreme anxiety and sleeplessness. David says something amazing, "I lie down and sleep. … I will not fear. … From the Lord comes deliverance." All this is followed by asking God to bless his people. David is able to move from his own personal pain and become outwardly-focused, asking God to bless his people. I believe these "selah" moments are filled with grace. These are moments we stop long enough to receive what God has for us.

> Receiving is one of the most difficult kinds of activity there is. To receive God is the chief work in contemplative prayer.[4]

The mistake many of us make is that we try to move forward in faith and trust in our own strength rather than waiting for God's enabling grace. After David asks God to bless his people, David finishes his psalm with "selah," taking the time to pause and reflect on what God has done.

The pattern is simply, express your problem, followed by a painful pause; turn your problem and pain into prayer, followed by a trusting pause. Receive the provision God has for you at the moment and then pause to rest in his love with a grateful heart.

Jesus
There is a similar pattern in Jesus' prayer in the Garden of Gethsemane before his death. He expresses, in brutal honesty, his despair in the presence of his heavenly Father and his closest friends.

> [Jesus] took Peter and the two sons of Zebedee along with him, and he began to be sorrowful and troubled. Then he said to them, "My soul is overwhelmed with sorrow to the point of death. Stay here and keep watch with me." (Matthew 26:37, 38)

This is followed by prayer.

> Going a little farther, he fell with his face to the ground and prayed, "My Father, if it is possible, may this cup be taken from me. Yet not as I will, but as you will."

> Then he returned to his disciples and found them sleeping. "Could you men not keep watch with me for one hour?" he asked Peter. "Watch and pray so that you will not fall into temptation. The spirit is willing, but the body is weak."

> He went away a second time and prayed, "My Father, if it is not possible for this cup to be taken away unless I drink it, may your will be done."

> When he came back, he again found them sleeping, because their eyes were heavy. So he left them and went away once more and prayed the third time, saying the same thing. (Matthew 26:39-44)

Jesus steps into a dialogue with God concerning the Father's will for him. He prays this way three times. Then, in the gospel of Luke, we find that,

> He withdrew about a stone's throw beyond them, knelt down and prayed, "Father, if you are willing, take this cup from me; yet not my will, but yours be done." An angel from heaven appeared to him and strengthened him. (Luke 22:41-43)

In the midst of Jesus' struggle, the Father sends an angel to strengthen him. He is given the grace, or provision, if you will, to move forward and embrace God's purposes for him.

Paul

The apostle Paul expresses this same kind of honesty in his own struggles. In 2 Corinthians, he explains the hardships he and his companions faced. He even goes so far as to say that he despaired of his life. He makes it clear that all of this was wrapped in prayer. Through this whole encounter, he not only experienced deliverance, he experienced transformation as he learned in a deeper way not to rely on himself but on God.

> We do not want you to be uninformed, brothers, about the hardships we suffered in the province of Asia. We were under great pressure, far beyond our ability to endure, so that *we despaired even of life.* Indeed, in our hearts we felt the sentence of death. But *this happened that we might not rely on ourselves but on God,* who raises the dead. He has delivered us from such a deadly peril, and he will deliver us. On him we have set our hope that he will continue to deliver us, as you help us by your prayers. Then many will give thanks on our behalf for the gracious favor granted us in answer to the prayers of many. (2 Corinthians 1:8-11, emphasis mine)

Though we have no record of Jesus or Paul journaling their struggles, what we do find is an emotional honesty, coupled with prayer that not only expresses their need, but also acts as a channel for God's grace and provision.

Keeping a spiritual journal can be a place of transformation. Again the pattern is simply, express your problem, followed by a painful pause, turn your problem and pain into prayer, followed by a trusting pause. Receive the provision God has for you at the moment and then pause to rest in his love with a grateful heart.

The nature of keeping a spiritual journal reveals how we process our understanding of who God is and who we are. There is no right way to journal; it is a very personal experience. You don't need to journal every day or even every week. Find a rhythm of journaling that fits your needs, season of life and personality. Don't worry about spelling or grammar. Journaling is a way to process your relationship with God. It is more important that you are honest than that you're a good writer.

Some people write in beautiful leather bound journals, other feel more comfortable in spiral notebooks. Personalize your journal to fit who you are. I also use my journal to do my pen and ink drawings. Find out what works best for you.

You might want to consider "harvesting your journal" at the end of the year.[5] This simply means you set aside some time to review over what you have written and then prayerfully reflect on your journey. Judy Davids, who originally taught me this concept, shares that she did this, only to discover that she was struggling with the same issues at the end of the year that she was struggling with at the beginning. This was a real wake-up call for her to be more intentional about getting help.

WALKING WITH GOD

"God created the heavens and the earth … and it was good."
Genesis 1:1, 31

Many forms of contemplative prayer focus on meditating on Scripture. There is also a rich heritage of meditating on God's first Bible, his creation. It is just as much an expression of God's love and character as the written Word. I was first introduced to walking meditation as a prayer form by Brother John Davies when I spent a month at the Benedictine monastery in Pecos, New Mexico. I had always enjoyed walking in nature, but I had never approached it as a prayer form before.

The Bible is rich with admonitions to pay attention to God's creation and listen to what he may be saying to us through nature.

> The heavens declare the glory of God; the skies proclaim the work of his hands. Day after day they pour forth speech; night after night they display knowledge. There is no speech or language where their voice is not heard. Their voice goes out into all the earth, their words to the ends of the world. (Psalm 19:1-4)

[Jesus said,] "Look at the birds of the air. ... See how the lilies of the field grow." (Matthew 6:26-28)

At the monastery we were taught to slowly and meditatively walk, being aware of our surroundings and, with a grateful heart, embracing God's creation with all our senses as his gift to us. As I continued this practice when I returned home, there was a real sense that I began to be energized when I took walks with this kind of prayerful attitude. It was as if God placed all this beauty around me as his gift to me, and what a tragedy for me to be too busy not to notice or appreciate it.

The real breakthrough came for me months after I had left the monastery and I was taking a walk late in the afternoon. It was early fall. I had been teaching on evangelism at a YWAM (Youth With a Mission) base in northern Germany. The classes were over and I was spending the weekend with some friends at a retreat center. As I was walking alone under a gray sky, I had this overwhelming sense that God was walking with me. Genesis 3:8 came to mind: "The Lord God ... was walking in the garden in the cool of the day." I immediately heard the voice of God on the inside of me: *I continue to walk in the midst of my creation.* With that insight came this new awareness that whether one is in the jungles of Thailand or on the mountains of northern India, along the coast of the Atlantic or even at Mitch Park in Edmond, Oklahoma – God is out walking in the midst of his creation. I was overwhelmed with the sense of holiness I felt at that moment. I could picture in my mind's eye, God taking a walk every day in the midst of his creation – and wanting to share it with us.

> I listen carefully to what God the Lord is saying, for he speaks peace to his faithful people. (Psalm 85:8, NLT)

Since that time, meditative walking has become a regular practice of mine. I walk with God in the midst of his creation, observing and enjoying with him what he has made. I don't spend the time planning my future or worrying about the past. I don't rehearse conversations I have had or plan to have. I reflect on what God might be saying to me, but more than that, I simply walk with God and live in the moment with him.

> Come and see what the Lord has done, the amazing things he has done on the earth. (Psalm 46:8, NCV)

I now see God's creation as his gift to me. It is his daily bread for my soul. Just as two lovers might enjoy a sunset or watch for falling stars together, it is the same with God. I simply walk with God in the midst of his creation, enjoying what God enjoys – the birds singing, the butterflies floating on the breeze, the wind rustling through the trees, the warmth of the sun on my skin.

CHAPTER 10

Through contemplative walking, I look at what I would otherwise overlook. I approach every walk with no agenda other than being with God and enjoying his company.

In the beginning, in order to slow down my thinking I would repeat a small prayer or phrase over in my mind. I would then coordinate it with my breathing and walking. I would pray something like, "I receive your love," or recite Psalm 23 or the Lord's Prayer in my mind. Other times I would reflect on what God had spoken to me through *lectio divina* and turn my meditation into a short breath prayer. Now that I have learned to be quiet on the inside, it is much easier to move into inner silence and simply walk with God. I just take in what I see, hear, touch, and sometimes taste; I respond with a grateful heart. There are times when he whispers in my heart, but most of the time we just walk together.

> Much of what is sacred is hidden in the ordinary, everyday moments of our lives. To see something of the sacred in those moments takes slowing down so we can live our lives more reflectively.[1]

As I unplug my iPod, I intentionally live in the now and simply walk with my senses wide open. I begin to see, hear, feel, even taste what God sees, hears, feels and tastes. I can't help but smile as I walk with God and enter into my beloved's joy. There is an awareness I carry now that the beauty of creation is God's gift to me. He made the world as beautiful as it is for his glory and for my enjoyment. To fail to notice and appreciate what God has for me because I am too busy or self-occupied is to lose the childlike wonder that marks true Christian spirituality.

> Then their eyes were opened and they recognized him [Jesus], and he disappeared from their sight. They asked each other, "*Were not our hearts burning within us while he talked with us on the road* and opened the Scriptures to us?" (Luke 24:31, 32, emphasis mine)

LECTIO DIVINA:
ENCOUNTERING
GOD IN THE BIBLE

"For the word of God is living and active. Sharper than any double-edged sword, it penetrates even to dividing soul and spirit, joints and marrow; it judges the thoughts and attitudes of the heart."
Hebrews 4:12

Lectio divina is a place. It is a place of rest and acceptance where you enter into heart-to-heart conversation with God. In time, it will become a place of transformation where the love of God touches you at the place of your deepest wounds and brings you into wholeness.

Lectio divina (lek-see-o de-vee-na) is an ancient prayer form that, for the first thousand years of church history, was an integral part of the church world. It is a devotional way of reading, meditating on and praying the Scriptures in a manner that enables the Word of God to penetrate deeply into our hearts. *Lectio divina* is built on the conviction that the Holy Spirit inspired the Bible and that the Holy Spirit continues to speak to us through the Scriptures. Through *lectio divina,* we can facilitate the word of God richly dwelling in us (Colossians 3:16).

Devotional reading of Scripture finds its roots in the Hebrew tradition. The early church adapted this practice and built on it. This practice began to be known as *lectio divina,* which is Latin for "divine reading." Saint Benedict, one of the early fathers of the monastic movement, set prayer, work and *lectio divina* as the three primary elements that gave rhythm to the daily life of Benedictine monks. Because of their dedication to the Scriptures and the other holy books of early Christianity, Benedictine monasteries were responsible for safeguarding much of the great literature during the Dark Ages. The Benedictines are also responsible for keeping alive the practice of *lectio divina* for the last 1500 years.

Lectio divina was further refined by Guigo II, a monk who lived in France during the twelve century. In his book, *Scala Claustralium (The Ladder of Monastics),* Guigo writes,

> One day I was engaged in physical work with my hands and I began to think about the spiritual tasks we humans have. While I was thinking, four spiritual steps came to mind: reading (lectio), mediation (meditatio), prayer (oratio), and contemplation (contemplatio). This is the ladder of monastics by which they are lifted up from the earth into heaven. There are only a few distinct steps, but the distance covered is beyond measure and belief since the lower part is fixed on the earth and its top passes through the clouds to lay bare the secrets of heaven.[1]

At one time, *lectio divina* was seen as four interchangeable parts, but after Guigo, the four parts began to be seen as four progressive steps: *lectio, meditatio, oratio* and *contemplatio.* For the purpose of training and making simple things even simpler, I have renamed the stages as Read, Reflect, Respond and Rest, and I have added a preparatory stage at the beginning, Ready, and an incarnational stage at the end, Return. I first heard Michael Palandro, pastor of the Vineyard Christian Fellowship of Houston, use this way of explaining *lectio divina,* and I liked it so much that I made it my own. I have also added journaling as part of the whole process. Journaling is central to integrating the word of God into our lives.

So here is my version of Guigo's ladder analogy.

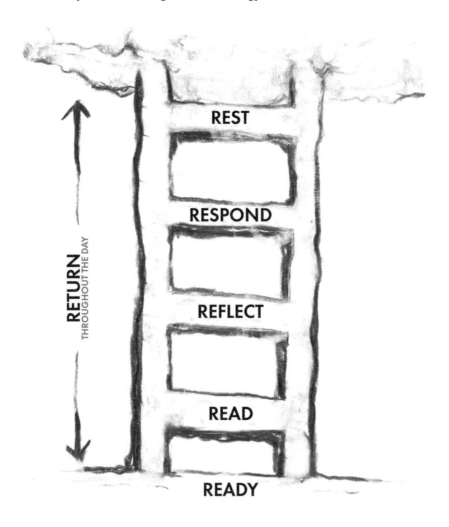

The steps, as I have written them, are only a guide. The point of *lectio divina* is to let God speak to you through his Word. Remember, your intention is to create a space in your life where you can encounter God and let him drive the conversation. You will find that there will be times when God will gently confront you and other times when God will simply pour out his strength and grace. There will also be times when God seems to be silent. But you will discover that God is always there to love you.

Don't be overly concerned with doing it "right." For instance, many people find it easier to begin with Rest (*contemplatio*) first. I have put time restraints on the different parts only as a guide for the beginner. Many people find it helpful to have these kinds of boundaries at the beginning. Once you have become comfortable with this model, you will find your own rhythm.

A Few Words About Journaling
There is a Chinese proverb that says, "Hearing, I forget; seeing, I remember; writing, I understand." Journaling is not traditionally taught as part of *lectio divina,* but I have found that it can be a real help in assisting you to process your own thoughts and respond to God's communication.

Keeping a prayer journal is different than keeping a diary. With a diary, you may simply write about your daily events and musings. With a prayer journal, you are using the activity of writing as a means of prayer and a way to process your inward journey with Christ. For instance, many of the Psalms are a type of spiritual journal of David's life. They record David's struggles, his pain, his doubts, disappointments, his insights from God and his victories.

Here are some things to keep in mind when keeping a journal:

- Purchase a spiral notebook or diary.
- Date your entries.
- Keep it personal and private.
- Keep it honest – write for yourself, not anyone else.
- Journal as needed – let it be an easy yoke.
- Take time to "harvest your journals" – periodically go back and review what you have written.[2]

When recording your thoughts and feelings about the passage and your conversation with God, don't be overly concerned with your spelling or punctuation. (You will not be graded.) Journaling is simply a way to keep a record of God's activity in your life. It also helps you to slow down so that you can better clarify your thoughts, prayers and reflections.

READY
(5 minutes)

Make yourself ready by, first of all, finding a quiet place where you will not be disturbed. If your intention is to make this prayer model a regular part of your devotional life, it's helpful to find a time and place that you can come to often. My personal practice is that I usually do *lectio divina* at the beginning of the day, early in the morning before the rest of the family gets up. The place you choose should be comfortable – my favorite is an overstuffed easy-chair in my living room. And because *lectio divina* involves having a conversation with God, I find that a cup of good dark coffee often enhances my prayer time. Conversation with God is developed out of an interior calm of resting, waiting and listening.

Once you're comfortable and calm, choose a brief passage of Scripture, no more than a couple of verses. Don't worry about spending too much time on such a small portion of Scripture. Because our intention is spiritual formation, rather than trying to race through as much of the Bible as we can, it is not unusual to spend a week or more with a single passage.

Then seek to be still and quiet – not only on the outside, but take the time to be still on the inside, too. Ask God to meet you during this time of prayer, and then reverently turn your attention to the passage you have selected.

READ
(5 minutes)

Lectio is Latin for "read." Read the text slowly, letting your awareness rest on each word, savoring it. *Lectio* is reverential reading, listening both in a spirit of silence and awe. You are listening for the still, small voice of God that will speak to you personally – not loudly, but intimately. Many times, I write out the verse to help me focus.

As you read, be aware of any particular word or phrase that draws your attention. Don't worry about whether or not this word is "from God," simply let yourself be drawn into that part of the Scripture. Once you have identified a word or phrase that caught your attention, you are ready to move to the next step.

REFLECT
(10 minutes)

Meditatio is Latin for "meditation." Meditate on this word or phrase, allowing it to engage you. Use your mind to analyze the word, to define what it means to you. Let the word engage you emotionally – use your imagination. Be aware of any emotions, memories or mental images that arrive within you as a result of your meditation. Begin to write down your thoughts. Concerning meditating on Scripture, Jan Johnson writes,

> Meditating is taking time to read a passage slowly and bringing all of our mind to the passage in quiet alertness. Instead of analyzing words, we *enter into* the passage, letting the words be spoken to us by the Holy Spirit to see what impact they will make on us. Meditation usually involves quieting oneself, reading the passage, rereading it, and then shutting our eyes to see what stands out to us today. Then we pray the Scripture so that we are dialoguing with God. God speaks to us in Scripture and we respond in prayer.[3]

Dallas Willard, writing about meditating, makes the observation,

> We withdraw into silence where we prayerfully and steadily focus upon it [Scripture]. In this way its meaning for us can emerge and form us as God works in the depths of our heart, mind, and soul. We devote long periods of time to this. Our prayer as we study meditatively is always that God would meet with us and speak specifically to us, for ultimately the Word of God is God speaking.[4]

After you have spent some time fully engaging your mind and emotions in meditation, you are ready to move to the next step.

RESPOND
(10 minutes)

Oratio is Latin for "prayer." During this part, respond to your meditation with prayer. Ask God why this word or phrase caught your attention – what is he trying to say to you? I usually write this question in my journal: *What are you saying to me?* Then I wait for an answer.

Dialogue with God about what you are feeling or hearing. Take time to listen. Don't try to censor what you think you are hearing from him, just go with it. You can go back later and determine if it lines up with Scripture and the character of God. This is a time to simply and honestly talk with God and yourself. It is during this step that transformation begins to take place.

Here's an example: Once when I was leading a prayer retreat, I had assigned everyone to spend the morning in solitude. I took the opportunity to practice *lectio divina,* and I was meditating on Psalm 23:4, "Even though I walk through the valley of the shadow of death, I will fear no evil, for you are with me; your rod and your staff, they comfort me."

I found myself drawn to the phrase, "I will fear no evil, for you are with me," so I spent some time meditating on these verses, thinking about the kinds of evil that still had a hold on me. The evil that seemed to have the strongest hold over me was the fear of disappointing others. When I asked God what he wanted to say to me, he responded, *You empower evil!* When I asked him how, he began speaking to me about my tendency to not face painful emotions and decisions, and that my ignoring of such evil was in fact empowering its hold on me.

In that moment, I did a fast rewind through my life, looking at event after event, where I empowered evil. When I asked God to deliver me, I saw an image of an authority figure from my youth who I felt I could never please. This figure seemed to be transposed over every relationship in my life. I then saw Christ behind this figure, with his arms stretched forth, inviting me to look past this person and receive God's comfort and power. I responded in prayer, and I began to experience a deep healing and transformation on the inside. I followed this by simply resting in God's love. This resting in God's love is the next step in *lectio divina*.

REST
(5 minutes)

Contemplatio simply means "contemplation," or wordless, quiet rest in the presence of God. The purpose of contemplation is not to get a word from God or any sort of divine revelation or experience. The purpose is to simply be attentive to the presence of God as he dwells within – to rest in him as he rest in you. There is a real mystery that happens when you sit quietly before God.

In this step, you are not trying to empty your mind. In fact, trying to empty your mind is impossible. What you are doing is focusing all your mental and emotional attention on God. In *Open Mind Open Heart,* Thomas Keating writes, "Receiving is one of the most difficult kinds of activity there is. To receive God is the chief work in contemplative prayer."[5]

Because of our culture and lifestyles, many Americans find that resting quietly before God can be a real challenge. For many, this step can be the most difficult and even seem to be a waste of time. So even though many contemplative writers encourage two 20-minute contemplative prayer times a day, for most of us this would be too much of a challenge.

> Contemplation is a strange new land ... where we learn a new language (silence), a new way of being (not to *do* but simply to *be*), where our thoughts and concepts, our imagination, senses and feelings are abandoned for faith in what is unseen and unfelt, where God's seeming absence (to our senses) is his presence, and his silence (to our ordinary perception) *is* his speech. ... To know our true selves is to know we are loved by God beyond all measure.[6]

If you find yourself struggling with quieting yourself on the inside, you might try using a short breath prayer. The one that I usually use is "I receive your love." Other times I turn my meditation or dialogue with God into a breath prayer. For example, if I'm reading the first verse of Psalm 23 and God is speaking to me about trusting him as my shepherd, I would simply turn my meditation into this breath prayer – breathe in, "You are," breathe out, "My shepherd."

If this sounds a bit mechanical, it's not. There is something wonderful that happens when you match your breath with prayer. These kinds of prayers help us to stay focused on what God is doing in our lives, as well as enable us to fulfill the apostle Paul's admonition to think about those things that are true, noble, right, pure, lovely, admirable, excellent and praiseworthy (Philippians 4:8).

There is a story of an old peasant who went every noon to the village church to pray. He would find a seat at the back of the church and simply sit and then get up and leave. One day, the priest asked, "Sir, is something troubling you?" "Oh no, Father," the old man replied. "I just look at God, and God looks at me."

RETURN
(throughout the day)

Return to your meditation throughout the day. The Word and Spirit must change us from the inside out. It is important that we are not like that person that the apostle James describes:

> Do not merely listen to the word, and so deceive yourselves. Do what it says. Anyone who listens to the word but does not do what it says is like a man who looks at his face in a mirror and, after looking at himself, goes away and immediately forgets what he looks like. (James 1:22-24)

It is not enough that you hear from God. It is not even enough to pray about it. God's intention is that his Word to us changes us into the image of Christ. We take the time to give ourselves to prayer in order to be changed. We want to move from simply doing Christian activity to becoming truly Christ-like.

Keep returning to the passage and your reflections on it throughout the day and throughout the week. Let the Word richly dwell within you; let it penetrate your soul and spirit. Be open for God to speak to you about your thoughts and the attitudes of your heart. Your intention must be that of being changed by the Word and Spirit of God – we don't change ourselves. In prayer, we create a space where we can be changed. Prayer does not change us – Christian spirituality teaches us that only God can change us. Without spiritual formation, *lectio divina* is simply a self-indulgent, religious exercise. It is important that your time in private prayer spills over into your public life.

It is the experience of many that God will give further insight if you continue to return to the same passage. A number of years ago, I was reading the first couple of verses of Matthew 5, "Now when he [Jesus] saw the crowds, he went up on a mountainside and sat down. His disciples came to him, and he began to teach them."

As I read this, I heard an invitation to sit with Jesus and let him teach me the lessons he taught his first disciples. It was an invitation to go through the Sermon on the Mount using *lectio divina*. I ended up spending three years, sitting with Jesus on the mountainside. To simply read through the verses takes less than an hour. To study the verses might take a little longer. To have the verses form you from within takes years, if not a lifetime.

Doing *Lectio Divina* With Others
Lectio divina can be practiced in a small group setting, as part of a family's devotional life, or as part of a couple's prayer time together.

When practiced in a small group, the facilitator gives a brief explanation of each step, including journaling. He then leads the group through each stage.

During the Read stage, have the participants take turns going around the room, reading the passage out loud a few times. Using different translations helps give the participants more places to hear a word that catches their attention.

During the Reflect and Respond stages, encourage the participants to write out their meditations and prayer dialogue.

After they've responded, invite the participants to read any of their insights that they feel comfortable sharing. The others in the group are free to offer affirmation, but they are not free to offer advice or correction. If what a person shares seems to be unbiblical, the facilitator might ask to speak to that person later in private.

Then, as a group, spend the last five minutes practicing the Rest stage together. This kind of community prayer exercise helps catalyze authenticity.

Lectio divina is also a wonderful prayer model for married couples. For years, my wife and I had struggled with praying together. We knew it was something that Christian couples should be doing together, but simply listening to each other's petitions seemed to fall far short of the spiritual unity we both wished to share with one another.

Now, when Dianna and I practice *lectio divina* together, we take turns reading the passage to each other, and then individually write out our meditations and prayer dialogue. We then share our insights and practice resting quietly before God together. It is a real joy to experience this kind of intimacy with each other in our spiritual lives.

SUMMARY

The practice of *lectio divina* is rather straightforward and easy to do, but don't let its simplicity fool you. I have done this exercise with middle-school and high-school students in a classroom; with hundreds of twenty-somethings at an abandoned horse racing track in East Germany; with 200 new pastors sitting cross-legged in a hot, dusty, crowded room in Andhra Pradesh, India; and with a room full of burned-out pastors and their wives in North America. And I am always surprised and awed by the different means God uses to communicate his love and transforming grace to his children.

SECTION 3
MAKING A LASTING CHANGE

A TRACK TO RUN ON

"I do all this for the sake of the gospel, that I may share in its blessings. Do you not know that in a race all the runners run, but only one gets the prize? Run in such a way as to get the prize. Everyone who competes in the games goes into strict training. They do it to get a crown that will not last; but we do it to get a crown that will last forever."
1 Corinthians 9:23 – 25

We need a pattern of spiritual disciplines that provides structure and direction for our growth into wholeness and holiness. The movement toward maturity and Christ-likeness is a process. You may experience the joy of revival and even have dramatic encounters with God. As wonderful as these experiences are, they don't replace the need for slow, steady movement toward God. We all need a plan for carrying out our decision to becoming more like Christ. We must develop a track to run on.

Dallas Willard says it this way:

> The crucial thing is that, as disciples, we have a plan for carrying out the decision we have made to devote ourselves to becoming like our Master and Lord – to increasingly living in the character and power of Christ. Disciples are those who, seriously intending to become like Jesus from the inside out, systematically and progressively rearrange their affairs to that end, under the guidance of the Word and the Spirit.[1]

Your own track or pattern should be an easy yoke – start small and increase your time as your appetite for God increases.

A good place to start is to develop your own sabbatical rhythm by building time into your life to pause, pray and play (see chapter 6).

PAUSE
To begin with, take a full day off each week. This is your Sabbath. It doesn't have to be a Sunday, just one full day of doing only things that you enjoy. For many of us our days off are simply days that we do the projects and run the errands we did not have time for during the week. This is not pausing. In fact Eugene Peterson, the author of *The Message* says it this way:

> An accurate understanding of Sabbath is prerequisite to its practice: It must be understood biblically, not culturally. A widespread misunderstanding of Sabbath trivializes it by designating it a "day off." "A day off" is a bastard Sabbath. Days off are not without benefits, to be sure, but Sabbaths they are not. However beneficial, they're not a true, but a secularized, Sabbath. The motivation is utilitarian: It makes us feel better. Relationships improve. We may even get more done on the six working days. The purpose is to restore strength, increase motivation, and keep performance incentives high.

> Sabbath means quit. Stop. Take a break. Cool it. The word itself has nothing devout or holy in it. It's a word about time, denoting our nonuse of it – what we usually call wasting time..[2]

This is a real challenge for families because Saturdays are now as busy, if not busier, than the other days of the week. For many, Saturdays are usually used for grocery shopping, cleaning house and doing chores. As with the other admonitions of Scripture, celebrating the Sabbath is there for our good and the good of our families.

Pausing means making sure you are getting enough rest physically and emotionally. We do this by setting aside time daily, if not weekly, to "find the dot." We need to decompress from the busyness of life and find the quiet time to ask and reflect "Where am I spiritually? Where am I emotionally? Where am I socially?" Use the examen as a prayer tool to help you answer these questions. Journal your feelings and any insight you get from God.

Then incorporate this rhythm on a larger scale. Once a month, try to get away for a long weekend. Once a year, take a non-working vacation.

PRAY
There are dozens of contemplative prayer models. In this season in my life, I rotate between using *lectio divina,* the examen, and contemplative walking.

Pray not as an activity, but as a place you go to in order to meet with God. A few minutes a day is a good start. Doing it once a week is better than not doing it at all. The important thing is that you start where you are. In time, prayer will become a place where you can be empowered, refreshed, challenged and made whole.

If this kind of prayer seems difficult, you might want to find a spiritual director or a spiritual formation group in your area that can provide support and structure.

PLAY
This is harder than it sounds. For those raised in the church, we may have a difficult time connecting having fun with Christian spirituality. Many of us know how to zone out, but learning how to play in a manner that refreshes and restores us is another matter.

Play looks different for different people. To be healthy, I encourage you to learn how to play alone, as well as with others. Play can be as simple as playing a board game with friends, reading good novels, fishing, gardening, or even going to yard sales on the weekends. The main difference between play and work is not so much the activity, it is whether you have to do it or you simply want to do it because you enjoy it and are refreshed from it.

Your pattern needs to be doable.
Building a healthy rhythm in your life will require change. Many of our lives are already maxed out. We would have a difficult time finding the time and energy to incorporate pause, pray and play into an already busy schedule. We are already juggling too many balls in the air as it is. Something has to give.

You have to realistically look at you schedule and ask yourself, *Is my inner life with Christ worth cultivating?* If you try to add contemplative spirituality as an appendage to an already busy life, you will fail. Growing into the image of

Christ must become central. In order to develop a healthy and growing spiritual life, more than likely, you will need to make some drastic changes.

Your pattern needs to be sustainable.
It is better to start out small and continue it over a period of time rather than to start out big and run out of gas in a week. Before starting any new program, you must ask yourself, *Is this sustainable?*

Your pattern needs to be profitable.
It has to work. It must never become discipline for discipline's sake. Are the times you spend pausing, praying, and playing forming you into a more Christ-like person? If not, then you need to re-examine what you are doing and why you are doing it.

Your pattern needs to be flexible.
Life happens. There will always be interruptions. On more than one occasion, Jesus' own prayer time was interrupted by other people's emergencies. That said, you need to be flexible, but not too flexible. You must value your soul enough to say, "No, not now." Your "No" must be stronger than others' "Yes."

Your pattern needs to be personal.
This is your pattern. Your pattern will look different than your spouse's or friends'. The kinds of things that give you life and feed your soul may look different. My wife is a storyteller. As we were looking for a pattern and a means to process our own inward journeys, we discovered that what worked for me did not really connect with her in the same way. We had to give each other permission to find out what worked best for us personally. Allow different kinds of prayer to morph into something that uniquely fits you. The purpose of *lectio divina* is not to do it perfectly. The purpose is to create a space in your life where you can encounter God and he can form you into the nature of Christ. Let your pattern and method be your own. My wife loves reading about other people's inner journeys via novels and memoirs. As she reads their story, she reflects on her own. My wife also enjoys processing her inner journey out loud and getting feedback from others. I tend to be more withdrawn and enjoy doing this in private. Your pattern needs to be personal.

Again, to echo the words of Dallas Willard,

> Disciplines for the spiritual life are places in which we meet Jesus to be taught by him, and he is our guide into how they are best practiced. *We should not be overly concerned about how others do them. In a very short time, Jesus will lead us into the practice that is best for us.*[3] (emphasis mine)

Your pattern needs to be rooted in community.

Christianity is a team sport. It is more like soccer than golf. All writers of the spiritual life warn of going it alone. We will discuss this more in the next chapter.

ENCOUNTERING GOD TOGETHER: PROCESSING YOUR INNER LIFE WITH OTHERS

"So in Christ we who are many form one body, and each member belongs to all the others."
Romans 12:5

"He who has himself as a spiritual director has a fool."
Ancient wisdom

"She who has her husband as a spiritual director has a fool."
Modern variation

To begin with, the modern variation of the ancient quote is by my wife, spoken somewhat tongue in cheek. As we were seeking to learn how to do contemplative prayer together as a couple, I would say to her, "*I am not your spiritual director, but if I was, I would tell you ...*" One day she responded back to me with the above modern variation. We both laughed and I learned how to keep my mouth shut.

Traditionally, when pursuing a contemplative prayer life, people are encouraged to find a spiritual director. For most people, this will not happen. There are a number of reasons for this. First of all, there are limited numbers of people who have been trained as spiritual directors (though the numbers are growing). Second, for many Christians this means stepping outside their faith tradition and this can be very difficult and unsettling for many people.

We must learn how to create a safe place in our congregations where people can process God's activity in their lives. We also must help people process through their life transitions.

In his book, *Satisfy Your Soul,* Bruce Demarest provided a great tool to help us understand the different ways we can wrap community around our contemplative prayer experience.[1] I have adapted his outline and added some insights of my own.

As you read through the suggestions, it moves from a very informal, unstructured, and sometimes reciprocal relationship to a more formal, structured, one-directional relationship.

BOOKS ON THE SPIRITUAL LIFE
Do not underestimate the value of those who have traveled this path before you. There is real benefit in reading the journey of others while processing your own. You don't have to agree with everything they write, but listening to them as they process their own journey can be beneficial.

Reading Sue Monk Kidd's book, *When the Heart Waits,* helped me understand my own journey better. Reading her next book, *The Dance of The Dissident Daughter,* gave me cause to question the inward journey I was on and challenged me to keep it Christ-centered.

Reading what Dallas Willard, Bruce Demarest, Jan Johnson and M. Robert Mulholland had to say on the spiritual life helped me lift the ancient contemplative practices out of the monastic culture and reinterpret them as an Evangelical.

Thomas Merton, Richard Foster and Henry Nouwen challenged me to go deeper.

Tony Jones' simple little book *Read, Think, Pray, Live* helped *lectio divina* come alive.

Thomas Keating's books on centering prayer helped me learn how to be still.

Sleeping with Bread by Dennis Linn, Sheila Fabricant Linn and Matthew Linn taught me how to do the examen.

These books and others have been companions to me. But it is important not to substitute reading these books for the actual practice of doing spiritual disciplines! To read a person's travel journal and not take the journey oneself is only spiritual voyeurism.

SPIRITUAL FRIEND

Finding others on a similar journey is a great benefit. A spiritual friend can be two or more Christians – who are on a relatively equal basis – who support, encourage and pray for one another. This can be as intimate as a husband and wife doing spiritual formation together. Having others you can share insights with is a tremendous blessing.

My friend and associate pastor, Jim Kimbrough, began taking a similar inward journey around the time I started mine. His insights, experiences and encouragement were very helpful to my own growth.

SPIRITUAL GUIDANCE

This is another informal helping ministry. It includes coming alongside a friend and talking about difficult issues, recommending a book, etc. This person can be a pastor or simply an older or more mature Christian.

SPIRITUAL FORMATION GROUP

This is a group of Christians who get together on a regular basis to practice a spiritual discipline, or discuss spiritual and personal issues. There is a sense of mutual accountability and self-disclosure. The group may or may not have a designated leader. Early in my development of my own contemplative prayer life, these kinds of groups were invaluable.

For those wanting to form spiritual formation groups, the following adaptations for group guidelines from Jan Johnson's book, *Savoring God's Word,* can be helpful. I have rewritten some of them.

Openness: I will be as candid and honest as I am able. I understand this group is a safe place in which I can admit strong emotions, confess faults and reveal insights that may seem outlandish.

Confidentiality: I will not tell anyone outside the group what someone else said in the group – not even spouses or absent members. I may tell someone else what I said, but not what someone else said.

Acceptance: I will avoid judging, giving advice or criticizing, even if it's only in my mind – "He is way off!" or "She is never going to plug into meditation." I will try to turn this self-talk into a prayer for the person and then focus on the passage in front of me.

Talking within the group: I understand that this is not a traditional discussion-oriented Bible study. I come together with others not to have extended conversation but for the community experience of seeking God. I will abide by instructions to comment only briefly. If something about the passage bothers me, I can discuss it with someone else later.

Wonder: I expect other group members to sense insights that are different from mine. God meets each of us in the places that still need to conform to the nature of Christ. For each of us, those places are different. I will make allowances for differences in temperament, timing and needs. Passages about metaphors and images resonate better with some people; others relate better to Bible characters; still others like the silence best. I will enjoy the wonder of how God speaks to each of us as individuals.

Privacy: No one is required to say anything. If I am unable to answer a question aloud because no answer comes to me or because I'm unwilling to reveal my answer to the group, I may say "pass" and offer no explanation.

Attentiveness: I will try to attend the group meetings and be open to the needs of others when I am there.

SPIRITUAL MENTORING

This is a more formal relationship in which a mature Christian offers another believer regular instruction, training and modeling in spiritual formation and ministry. This is someone who has taken the journey and is willing to share their wisdom and insight with you.

Two counselors were instrumental in my own growth. Both of these women were trained in the disciplines of counseling and psychology. They had worked through the dark nights of their own souls and were familiar with the means God uses to bring his children to wholeness.

My friend Judy Davids helped me develop my own sabbatical rhythm.

Dr. Donna McCoy helped my wife and I think through how to structure a three-month sabbatical in Europe.

SPIRITUAL DIRECTOR

This is a structured ministry in which a gifted and experienced Christian helps another believer grow in relationship and obedience to Christ. The spiritual director is usually gifted in discernment, wisdom and knowledge; in fact, many see that the role of a spiritual director is a gift given by the Holy Spirit. Their task is to help people process their relationship with Christ. This is a specialized ministry, and if you are seeing a spiritual director, some kind of financial compensation should be given.

The spiritual disciplines come to us from a Christian culture that understood and embraced community. Contemplative prayer is meant to be practiced in the context of mutual submission and community.

Changing a long-time behavior pattern takes a lot of energy and discipline, especially at first. Having people who cheer you on and walk with you is often the difference between success and failure.

APPENDICES

LECTIO DIVINA: THEMES

If you are going to integrate *lectio divina* into your prayer life, where do you start? In one sense, it does not really matter. The entire Bible is inspired by God. If there is an area in your life God wants to speak to, he can speak to it whether you are reading in the Psalms or the Epistles. One of the things you will discover is that God will take you through seasons where he will continue to bring up the same issues until he is satisfied that you are on your way to being changed.

If you are looking for a place to start, I would encourage you to begin with passages that are already your favorites and see what else God might want to say. The Psalms are a natural for *lectio divina,* as well as John's letters. Ask God to show you where to start.

Another way to approach this is to intentionally approach *lectio divina* as a means of incarnating Biblical truths into known areas (quadrant two of the Johari Window, or your private self) that you may want to grow in. *Lectio divina* is a good prayer model for the integration of Biblical truth into the life of a believer. Again, the purpose of *lectio divina* is not to cover as much Scripture as possible. Your goal is the inner formation of your soul to the character and nature of Jesus.

You may want to spend some time working through the Sermon on the Mount with the purpose of becoming the kind of "blessed" person that Jesus is calling you to become. While working on larger passages of Scripture, such as the Sermon on the Mount, give yourself permission to take a break and focus on another section. For a season, when I was doing *lectio divina* alone, I would use the Sermon on the Mount. The days that I would practice with my wife, we would go through 1 John.

If there are areas in your life that you are struggling with, many times practicing *lectio divina* around those themes and waiting for God to speak to you personally is helpful. I have written out a number of themes you might want to spend some time around. As you pick a theme, remember to work through only a verse or two at a time.

God's Love
>   Isaiah 62:5
>   John 3:16
>   Ephesians 2:4 – 7
>   1 John 2:1 – 3
>   1 John 4:7 – 19

The Holy Spirit
>   John 14:16 – 17
>   John 7:38 – 39
>   John 16:13
>   Romans 8:15
>   Romans 8:26 – 27
>   Acts 2:17 – 18

Rest
>   Genesis 2 – 3
>   Exodus 20:8 – 11
>   Leviticus 29 – 31
>   Jeremiah 50:6
>   Psalm 23
>   Mark 2:27 – 28

Hearing the Voice of God
>   John 10:27 – 30
>   Jeremiah 31:33 – 34

Humility
>   Matthew 18:1 – 5
>   Philippians 2:3 – 11

Identification with the Poor and Disenfranchised
Isaiah 58:2 – 8
Luke 4:18 – 19
Matthew 25:34 – 40
1 Timothy 6:17 – 18

God and Nature
Psalm 8:1 – 9
Psalm 19:1 – 4
Matthew 6:26

Fruitfulness
Psalm 1:1 – 3
John 15:1 – 5
2 Peter 1:3 – 10

The Bible
2 Timothy 3:16
1 John 2:14
Colossians 3:16
Hebrews 4:12 – 13
Proverbs 4:20 – 23
Psalm 119:9 – 18

Forgiveness
Matthew 5:44 – 45
Romans 12:17 – 21
Luke 6:35 – 38
1 John 1: 8 – 9

Patience
James 1:2 – 4
James 5:7 – 8
Galatians 6:9
Hebrews 6:12
Hebrews 10:36

False Self / True Self
    John 12:23 – 26
    Romans 6:3 – 11
    Colossians 3:5 – 11

Meditation
    Joshua 1:7 – 9
    Psalm 1:1 – 3
    Psalm 119:14 – 16
    Proverbs 4:20 – 23

Centering Prayer and the Indwelling Christ
    John 11:25 – 27
    John 11:55 – 57
    Galatians 2:20
    Colossians 1:26 – 28
    1 John 4:15 – 17
    Revelations 3:19 – 21

Solitude
    Mark 1:35 – 38
    Mark 6:30 – 32
    Matthew 14:22 – 24

LECTIO DIVINA: OUTLINE

01 READY

Find a place where you can be quiet and undisturbed.
Choose a brief passage of Scripture.
Ask God to meet you during this time of prayer.
You may want to journal *lectio divina*.

02 READ

(5 minutes)
Read the passage slowly, letting your awareness rest on each word.
Listen for the still small voice of God.
Be aware of any word or phrase that catches your attention.

03 REFLECT

(10 minutes)
Meditate on the word or phrase that caught your attention.
Use your mind to analyze the word or phrase.
Be aware of any emotion or memories the word may stir up.

04 RESPOND

(10 minutes)
Respond to the word.
Ask God why this word caught your attention. What is he trying to say to you?
Dialogue with God about what you are feeling or hearing.
Take time to listen.

05 REST

(5 minutes)

Rest in God's presence. Wordless, quiet rest in the presence of God is called "contemplation."

06 RETURN

Keep returning to the passage and your reflection.

Keep returning with the intention of integrating the word into your life.

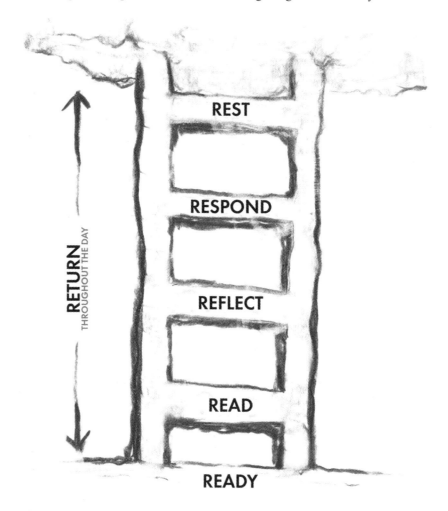

APPENDIX 3
RECOMMENDED RESOURCES FOR THE INNER LIFE

The following are books and resources that proved to be companions to me as I learned how to process through my own midlife transition and recover from burnout. As beneficial as these books and resources are, nothing can replace having loving and understanding people you can talk to and process life with.

But the most important source of strength, life, and true transformation came out of that sacred place of prayer. As helpful as other's insights are, nothing can replace hearing from God and receiving his grace and power to change.

Judy Davids is a missionary, professional counselor, retreat director and educator. She is married to theologian Peter Davids. She has worked with burned-out pastors for several years and has directed Pastor's Sabbath Retreats in Austria, the United States and Canada. She is an ordained Vineyard pastor and has built lay counseling ministry and recovery groups in several churches. She presently lectures in the psychology department at St. Stephen's University, New Brunswick, Canada. God used Judy to challenge my destructively busy lifestyle and helped me to develop my own sabbatical rhythm. She is a friend and mentor. Along with her lectures, she continues to lead retreats and does personal counseling. Judy can be reached at: judy@davidsnet.ws

The Pecos Benedictine Community is nestled in the Sangre de Cristo Mountain. It is located twenty-five miles east of Santa Fe, New Mexico. The monks and sisters of Our Lady of Guadalupe Abbey continue the long history of Benedictine life going back to Saint Benedict, one of the founders of monasticism in the Western world (AD 480-547). From its very inception, the Pecos Monastery has served as a center for retreats, teaching and church renewal. It is here that I received training to be a spiritual director. The prayerful atmosphere in the monastery, the kindness of the monks and sisters, and the beauty of the location was like oxygen to my soul. Their website is http://www.pecosmonastery.org

Dallas Willard is one of the most respected writers on the spiritual life of our generation. His books *Hearing God, The Spirit of the Disciplines, The Divine Conspiracy,* and *Renovation of the Heart* are classics. His website, www.dwillard.org has a number of very helpful articles on the spiritual life. Willard's writings helped me place contemplative prayer in the context of spiritual formation.

M. Robert Mulholland, Jr. is a professor of New Testament at Asbury Theological Seminary. In his books *Invitation To A Journey* and *The Deeper Journey,* he discusses the false selves we hide behind and helps the reader discover the true self that is found in Christ.

Richard Foster is a Quaker. He is an author of several bestselling books, including *Celebration of Discipline, Streams of Living Water,* and *Prayer.* He is founder of Renovare, an movement committed to renewal of the church. Foster has a real gift for making ancient spirituality and wisdom accessible to modern readers.

Jan Johnson is an Evangelical writer, retreat leader and Bible teacher. Her books *Savoring God's Word* and *When the Soul Listens* are good, biblically-based introductions to contemplative prayer.

Tony Jones' books are easy to read and provide a good introduction to contemplative spirituality. Jones is sometimes identified as part of the Emergent Church movement. When presenting different contemplative prayer models, he provides a brief historical overview, coupled with biblical theology and practical application. Two of his books that are favorites of mine are *Divine Intervention: Encountering God through the Ancient Practice of Lectio Divina* (formerly titled *Read, Think, Pray, Live*) and *The Sacred Journey.*

David G. Benner is a psychologist, spiritual director and retreat leader. He is the author of many books including *Sacred Companions, Surrender to Love* and *The Gift of Being Yourself. The Gift of Being Yourself* connected the dots for me in understanding that healthy Christian spirituality involves not only knowing God, but knowing oneself.

Thomas Keating and **M. Basel Pennington** are both Benedictine monks. Keating's books, *Open Heart, Open Mind* and *Intimacy with God,* along with Pennington's book, *Centering Prayer* are modern classics on the ancient practice of contemplative prayer. Both of their books provide historical perspective,

Christian theology and practical application. Their approach is decidedly Catholic. Keating's website, www.centeringprayer.com is a great resource.

Cynthia Bourgeault is an Episcopal priest. She is a retreat and conference leader and a writer on spiritual life. Her book, *Centering Prayer and Inner Awakening* is easy to read and a must for anyone interested in centering prayer. She does a great job of building on Thomas Keating's works and offering a fresh perspective.

Dr. Bruce Demarest is a professor at Denver Seminary. He has written books on psychology, theology and contemplative prayer. His book, *Satisfy Your Soul,* is a great overview and introduction to contemplative prayer. Demarest has an evangelical mind and a contemplative heart. I use *Satisfy Your Soul* as a must-read when introducing evangelicals to contemplative prayer.

Janet O. Hagbert is a public speaker, spiritual director and social activist. The late **Robert A. Guelich** was a professor of New Testament at Fuller Theological Seminary. Their book, *The Critical Journey* is one of the best books written on how God forms and shapes us through the seasons of our lives. I was introduced to this book through the writings of Bruce Demarest. If you want to understand what spiritual formation looks like over a lifetime, this is an extremely helpful resource.

Leland Ryken is a professor of English at Wheaton College. He has authored more than twenty books. His book, *Redeeming the Time: A Christian Approach to Work and Leisure,* was a life saver. I had a theology for work and activity. I needed to develop an Evangelical theology for leisure. Ryken provides insights drawn from the social sciences, literature, history, theology and biblical studies. This book is well written and makes a convincing argument for intentionally developing a life that is marked by both work and leisure.

Peter Scazzero pastors a large, multiracial church in Queens, New York. His book *Emotionally Healthy Spirituality* argues that you can't be spiritually mature while remaining emotionally immature. He provides a biblical integration of emotional health and the classical practices of contemplative prayer. This is a good book for pastors.

Fred Lehr is a pastor in the Evangelical Lutheran Church. His book, *Clergy Burnout* is written for pastors. Lehr makes the connection between burnout and codependency. In his book he discusses how codependent pastors build codependent church systems to survive. His was a painful book to read. It is recommended for those who think they may be codependent or who may be moving toward burnout.

Sue Monk Kidd has become a best selling novelist with the publication of *The Secret Life of Bees* and *The Mermaid Chair.* Her earlier works were decidedly Christian. Her book *When the Heart Waits* is her account of her journey from evangelicalism to contemplative spirituality. This book was a real inspiration and companion for me as I was trying to understand what God was doing in my life. Her following book, *The Dance of The Dissident Daughter,* is her journey from orthodox Christianity into divine feminism. This book was a real shock and caused me to reevaluate my own inward journey. In the end, it helped me recognize the possible pitfalls and dangers of taking the inward journey. It became clear that Jungian psychology had a stronger pull on her than biblical spirituality. Both my wife and I were very moved by Sue Monk Kidd's honesty and courage. Though I don't agree with all of her convictions, I do admire her honesty. I would recommend *When the Heart Waits* to those moving through a midlife transition.

James Finley is a former Trappist monk who studied closely with Thomas Merton. He is now a clinical psychologist. He has written a number of books on the contemplative life. His book, *Merton's Palace of Nowhere: A Search for God Through Awareness of the True Self* is a good introduction to Thomas Merton's approach to prayer and contemplation. Thomas Merton is one of the major spiritual thinkers of our time.

Dennis Linn, Sheila Fabricant Linn, and **Matthew Linn** wrote a wonderful, easy- to-read book called *Sleeping With Bread.* This charming book is a great modern adaptation of Ignatian spirituality. They provide a contemporary, easy model for doing the examen. This book is a must for those wanting to recognize God's activity in their everyday lives.

N O T E S

Chapter 1 An Invitation and a Warning

1. Dallas Willard, *The Spirit of the Disciplines: Understanding How God Changes Lives,* (HarperCollins Publishers, 1988), p. ix

2. Cynthia Bourgeault, *Centering Prayer and Inner Awakening* (Cowley Publications, 2004), p. 67

3. Dallas Willard, *The Spirit of the Disciplines: Understanding How God Changes Lives,* (HarperCollins Publishers, 1988), p. ix

4. Richard Foster, *Prayer: Finding the Heart's True Home* (HarperCollins Publishers, 1992), p. 6

Chapter 2 Spiritual Disciplines as a Place to Encounter Jesus

1. Richard Foster, *Prayer: Finding the Heart's True Home* (HarperCollins Publishers, 1992)

2. John Wimber, *"Revisiting Vineyard Priorities: Worship"* (Equipping the Saints, Volume 6, Number 3, Summer 1992)

3. David G. Benner, *The Gift of Being Yourself: The Sacred Call to Self-Discovery,* (InterVarsity Press, 2004), p. 64

4. Richard Foster, *Celebration of Discipline: The Path to Spiritual Growth* (HarperCollins Publishers, 1978)

5. Dallas Willard, *The Spirit of the Disciplines: Understanding How God Changes Lives,* (HarperCollins Publishers, 1988) pp. 156-191

6. Dallas Willard, "How Does the Disciple Live?" (www.dwillard.org)

7. Jan Johnson, *When The Soul Listens: Finding Rest and Direction in Contemplative Prayer* (NavPress, 1999), p. 37

8. M. Robert Mulholland Jr., *Invitation to a Journey: A Road Map for Spiritual Formation,* (InterVarsity Press, 1993) p. 12

9. M. Robert Mulholland Jr., *Invitation to a Journey: A Road Map for Spiritual Formation,* (InterVarsity Press, 1993) p. 37

10. M. Robert Mulholland Jr., *Invitation to a Journey: A Road Map for Spiritual Formation,* (InterVarsity Press, 1993) p. 41

11. Thelma Hall, *Too Deep For Words: Rediscovering Lectio Divina* (Paulist Press, 1988), p. 49-50

Chapter 3 Spiritual Disciplines as a Place to Encounter Ourselves

1. David G. Benner, *The Gift of Being Yourself: The Sacred Call to Self-Discovery,* (InterVarsity Press, 2004), p. 53-54

2. James Finley, *Merton's Palace of Nowhere: A Search for God Through Awareness of the True Self,* (Ave Maria Press, 1978), p. 99

3. Thomas Merton, *New Seeds of Contemplation,* (New Direction Books, 1972), p. 31

Chapter 4 Our Spiritual Journey

1. Janet O. Hagberg and Robert A. Guelich, *The Critical Journey: Stages in the Life of Faith,* (Sheffield Publishing Company, 2005)

2. Dr. Bruce Demarest, *Soul Guide: Following Jesus as Spiritual Director,* (NavPress, 2003)

3. Peter Scazzero, *Emotionally Healthy Spirituality: Unleash a Revolution in Your Life in Christ,* (Integrity Publishers, 2006)

4. Sue Monk Kidd, *When the Heart Waits: Spiritual Direction for Life's Sacred Questions,* (HarperCollins Publishers, 1990)

5. M. Robert Mulholland Jr., *Invitation to a Journey: A Road Map for Spiritual Formation,* (InterVarsity Press, 1993)

6. M. Robert Mulholland Jr., *Invitation to a Journey: A Road Map for Spiritual Formation,* (InterVarsity Press, 1993), p. 85

7. Sue Monk Kidd, *When the Heart Waits: Spiritual Direction for Life's Sacred Questions,* (HarperCollins Publishers, 1990), p. 52

8. Sue Monk Kidd, *When the Heart Waits: Spiritual Direction for Life's Sacred Questions,* (HarperCollins Publishers, 1990), p. 151

9. Dr. Bruce Demarest, *Satisfy Your Soul: Restoring the Heart of Christian Spirituality* (NavPress, 1999), p. 212

10. M. Robert Mulholland Jr., *Invitation to a Journey: A Road Map for Spiritual Formation,* (InterVarsity Press, 1993), pp. 94-95

Chapter 5 **Contemplative Prayer as a Place**

1. Frank L. Baum, *The Wizard of Oz,* (1900)

2. James Finley, *Merton's Palace of Nowhere: A Search for God through Awareness of the True Self,* (Ave Maria Press, 1978), p.47

3. M. Robert Mulholland Jr., *Invitation to a Journey: A Road Map for Spiritual Formation,* (InterVarsity Press, 1993), p. 20

Chapter 6 **Sabbatical Rhythm**

1. Judy Davids, Pastor's Sabbath Retreat (September 21 - October 1, 2004; September 11 - 22, 2007)

2. Dr. Bruce Demarest, *Satisfy Your Soul: Restoring the Heart of Christian Spirituality* (NavPress, 1999), p. 126

3. Leonard Doohan, *Leisure: A Spiritual Need* (Ave Maria Press, 1990), p. 46

4. Dallas Willard, *Renovation of the Heart: Putting on the Character of Christ,* (NavPress, 2002), p. 175

5.Robert Clinton (Leadership development lectures, Southwestern Christian University Graduate School, 1999)

6. Dallas Willard, *Renovation of the Heart: Putting on the Character of Christ,* (NavPress, 2002), p. 159

7. Dallas Willard, *Renovation of the Heart: Putting on the Character of Christ* (NavPress, 2002) pp. 175-176

8. Peter Scazzero, *Emotionally Healthy Spirituality: Unleash a Revolution in Your Life in Christ,* (Integrity Publishers, 2006) p. 56

9. Leland Ryken, *Redeeming the Time: A Christian Approach to Work & Leisure* (Baker Books, 1995) p. 64

Chapter 7 **Centering Prayer: Resting in God**

1. Adele Ahlberg Calhoun, *Spiritual Disciplines Handbook: Practices That Transform Us,* (InterVarsity Press, 2005), p. 208

2. M. Basil Pennington, *Centering Prayer: Renewing an Ancient Christian Prayer Form,* (Doubleday, 1980) p. 18

3. M. Basil Pennington, *Centering Prayer: Renewing an Ancient Christian Prayer Form,* (Doubleday, 2001) pp. 26-27

4. Tony Jones, *The Sacred Way: Spiritual Practices for Everyday Life,* (Zondervan, 2004) p. 74

Chapter 8 **The Examen: Paying Attention to God**

Chapter 9 **Journaling as a Place of Prayer and Transformation**

1. Adele Ahlberg Calhoun, *Spiritual Disciplines Handbook: Practices That Transform Us,* (InterVarsity Press, 2005), p. 57

2. David G. Benner, *The Gift of Being Yourself: The Sacred Call to Self-Discovery,* (InterVarsity Press, 2004), p. 56

3. Jan Johnson, *When The Soul Listens: Finding Rest and Direction in Contemplative Prayer* (NavPress, 1999), p. 45

APPENDIX 3

4. Thomas Keating, *Open Mind, Open Heart: The Contemplative Dimension of the Gospel,* (The Continuum International Publishing Group Inc, 1992), p. 71

5. Judy Davids, Pastor's Sabbath Retreat (September 21 – October 1, 2004; September 11 – 22, 2007)

Chapter 10 Walking with God

1. Ken Gire, *Seeing What Is Sacred: Becoming More Spiritually Sensitive to the Everyday Moments of Life,* (W Publishing Group, 2006), p. 19

Chapter 11 Lectio Divina: Discovering A Place Called Prayer

1. Tony Jones, *The Sacred Way: Spiritual Practices for Everyday Life,* (Zondervan, 2004) p. 49-50

2. Judy Davids, Pastor's Sabbath Retreat (September 21 – October 1, 2004; September 11 – 22, 2007)

3. Jan Johnson, *Savoring God's Word: Cultivating the Soul-Transforming Practice of Scripture Meditation,* (NavPress, 2004), p. 22

4. Dallas Willard, *The Spirit of the Disciplines: Understanding How God Changes Lives,* (HarperCollins Publishers, 1988) p. 177

5. Thomas Keating, *Open Mind, Open Heart: The Contemplative Dimension of the Gospel,* (The Continuum International Publishing Group Inc, 1992), p. 71

6. Thelma Hall, *Too Deep For Words: Rediscovering Lectio Divina* (Paulist Press, 1988), p. 49

Chapter 12 A Track to Run On

1. Dallas Willard, "How Does the Disciple Live?" (www.dwillard.org)

2. ed. H.B. London, Jr., *Refresh, Renew, Revive* (Tyndale House Pub, 1996), Eugene Peterson, "The Pastor's Sabbath," pp. 81 – 87

3. Dallas Willard, "How Does the Disciple Live?" (www.dwillard.org)

Chapter 13 **Encountering God Together**

1. Dr. Bruce Demarest, *Satisfy Your Soul: Restoring the Heart of Christian Spirituality* (NavPress, 1999), p. 195

ABOUT THE AUTHOR

Charles Bello is a writer, pastor to pastors, a trained spiritual director, retreat director, and teacher. He has trained pastors, missionaries and lay leaders in more than 15 nations. He and his wife, Dianna have six children and live in Edmond, Oklahoma.

For more information, contact Charles at www.coachingsaints.com

A NEW BOOK BY CHARLES BELLO

Coaching Saints

empowered ministry and contemplative spirituality

A saint is classically defined as someone who performs a miracle and lives an extraordinary holy life. As disciples of Jesus, we are called to do both. We are called to do the works that Jesus did and live the life that Jesus lived. In this groundbreaking book, Charles explores how we can learn to partner with the Holy Spirit to do the supernatural works of Christ, while at the same time cooperate with God to live in the holiness that is to mark every saint.

OTHER BOOKS BY HGM PUBLISHING

Passion for the Heart of God
Making His Heart Completely Yours
John Willis Zumwalt

"Today a revolution is needed; a revolution that needs to take place in the Church, not only in America, but around the world; a revolution that gets people's focus off of themselves and on to God and His glory; a revolution where once again, man will serve God, not God serve man; a revolution that will move the Church to take our Father's glory to all of the nations on the face of the earth. In John's insightful book, Passion for the Heart of God, John gives a creative challenge to the Church to pursue God's heart to the ends of the earth. His stories are fresh, energizing and easy to read, but best of all, he holds nothing back. John challenges us all to become a part of the needed revolution. I highly encourage anyone in the Body of Christ to read this book."

— Bob Sjogren, president, UnveilinGLORY and author, Unveiled at Last

Complete in Him to Complete the Task
James Lee West

"How can we ever hope to have a passion for the lost if there is no passion for Jesus that causes us to leave behind everything that would compete for love and loyalty? The call of Jesus is that we follow Him completely. Unless we are complete in Him, the very idea of completing the commission to go into all the world and make disciples will always remain a mythical part of mere Christian teaching."

— from Complete in Him

E N C O U R A G E
O T H E R S T H R O U G H
T H I S B O O K

Call today to order your copies of *Prayer as a Place* or other HGM Publishing materials:

405-737-9446

Or complete the following form and mail it, with payment, to:

Heart of God Ministries
ATTN: HGM Publishing
3720 S. Hiwassee Rd.
Choctaw, OK 73020

Suggested donations:
$15 each
3-10 copies at $12 each
11 or more copies at $10 each

Please make checks payable to Heart of God Ministries.

Request for Materials

☐ Yes! Please send me _____ copies of *Prayer as a Place* at $ _____ each.

☐ Yes, God is calling me to go! Please send me more information about missionary training at Beautiful Feet Boot Camp.

☐ Yes, I want to receive *Frontlines* magazine! Please add me to HGM's mailing list.

Please Print

Name _____

Address _____

City _____ State _____ Zip Code _____

Country _____ Telephone _____

Email _____

Total payment enclosed: $ _____